BERLIN'S
THIRD
SEX

MAGNUS HIRSCHFELD

BERLIN'S THIRD SEX

*Translated from the German and
with an afterword by James J. Conway*

RIXDORF EDITIONS BERLIN 2017

Berlin's Third Sex by Magnus Hirschfeld was first published in German as
Berlins drittes Geschlecht by Verlag von Hermann Seemann Nachfolger
in Berlin and Leipzig, undated (1904), as Volume 3 of the *Großstadt-
Dokumente* (Metropolis Documents) series.

What People Should Know About the Third Sex by Magnus Hirschfeld was
first published in German as *Was muss das Volk vom dritten Geschlecht
wissen!* by Verlag von Max Spohr in Leipzig, 1901, and attributed to
the Wissenschaftlich-humanitaren Comitee (Scientific-Humanitarian
Committee).

This translation, afterword and anthology © 2017 James J. Conway

Berlin's Third Sex
first published Rixdorf Editions, Berlin, 2017

Design by Cara Schwartz

Printed by Totem.com.pl, Inowrocław, Poland

ISBN: 978-3-947325-02-3 (e-book 978-3-947325-03-0)

RixdorfEditions.com

CONTENTS

BERLIN'S THIRD SEX

'The great vanquisher of all prejudice is not humanity, but science.'

AUTHOR'S FOREWORD

When Hans Ostwald, publisher of the *Metropolis Documents*[1], asked me to work on a volume that would address the lives of homosexuals in Berlin, I felt it was a challenge I could not shrug off.

While the results of my research into the field of homosexuality have only been published in specialist journals to date, particularly in the *Yearbook For Sexual Intermediaries*[2], it has long been clear to me that knowledge of an area that is intertwined with the interests of so many families, of every class, would not and could not remain forever confined in the closed community of specialists or academic circles.

That being said, it is certainly prudent that the presentation of such a difficult issue in a popular science setting be left to those who have attained the necessary qualifications and skills by virtue of extensive scientific research and experience, and on the basis of close examination.

In this work I have tried to reflect, as authentically

and comprehensively as possible, Berlin's 'third sex' as the common, if not entirely appropriate designation refers to it. While not identifying physical locations too closely, I tried – without whitewashing, but also avoiding the darkest shades – to depict everything exactly as it is, largely as I have perceived it for myself, but to a lesser extent relying on the testimony of trustworthy sources; it gives me pleasure at this point to thank them for their trust in me.

Many readers will discover in the midst of their familiar world a new world opening up, the extent and customs of which may fill them with astonishment.

One sometimes hears the concern that writing about homosexuality for a mass audience might itself serve as 'propaganda'. Insofar as one strives to arrive at a fair judgment of the homosexual, this fear is baseless. The danger simply is not there. The advantages of normal sexual life, including the expression it finds in the happiness of the family – to name just one among many – are so pronounced, and the disadvantages arising from the homosexual condition so extreme, that if a shift in orientation were indeed possible it would surely be exercised by the homosexual rather than the normally sexed.

However, on this point scientific observation is in accord with the personal experience of a great number of people – such a transformation is impossible, because nothing is so aptly and inseparably tailored to the character and essence of a person as the orientation of the romantic and sexual drive so crucial to overall individuality.

Whether, and to what degree the deeds of homosexuals should be considered in light of such terms as guilt and crime; whether, and to what degree their prosecution appears appropriate or necessary; the extent to which this is even possible – on these points I would prefer to let my readers make up their own minds at the end of my report.

Charlottenburg, 1 December 1904[3]
Dr Magnus Hirschfeld

BERLIN'S THIRD SEX

If one wished to produce a vast portrait of a world-class city like Berlin, penetrating the depths rather than merely dwelling on the surface, one could scarcely ignore the impact of homosexuality, which has fundamentally influenced both the shading of this picture in detail and the character of the whole.

While it is hardly likely that there are more homosexuals born in Berlin than in small towns or the hinterlands, it stands to reason that, whether consciously or unconsciously, those who deviate in undesirable ways from the majority gravitate to places where they might live less conspicuously, and less beleaguered, in the amplitude and mutability of the many. It is precisely this that makes a metropolis so attractive and distinctive, that individuals are not subject to their neighbours' surveillance as they are in smaller localities, where the circles are closed, so too minds and senses. In such places it is easy to monitor when, where and with whom the neighbours eat, drink, stroll and sleep – and monitor they do, avidly – while in Berlin those in the front of an apartment building often have no idea who is living in the rear block of the same building[4], let alone what those inhabitants get up to. And yet there are buildings here that contain a hundred households, a thousand people.

That which is hidden from the uninitiated in the metropolis can be all the more easily discovered by the initiate, because it is far less constrained.

Any well-informed person will soon notice that the streets and pleasure spots of Berlin boast not just men and women in the accepted sense, but frequently also those who differ not just in their behaviour, but often their appearance as well, such that alongside the masculine and feminine one can almost speak of a third sex.

This expression was in common currency as far back as ancient Rome, and while I do not find it particularly suitable, it is at least better than the word homosexual (same-sex) which is so often used today, because this term gives credence to the widely-held assumption that wherever a number of homosexuals gather, sexual acts are in preparation if not in progress, an assumption that in no way accords with the facts.

So when this study mentions homosexuals, one should not think of any type of sexual act. Where they do occur they elude observation not just because of their illegal status, but most especially because of the natural sense of shame and morality which is as pronounced in the homosexual as in the normally sexed; these acts are by no means the main focus, and are often absent altogether. What matters here is the essence of the uranian – and in this text we echo Ulrichs[5] in using this name for those with homosexual sentiments – and that his behaviour toward the male and female sexes derives from the attractions and antipathies within his nature.

But even for those who recognise many typical qualities of the uranian, a great deal still remains concealed, whether because they, and this is by no means rare, bear no readily identifiable signs, or because they play out the comedy – or more likely tragedy – of their life with great skill, able to adapt themselves and all their habits to those of normal people, prudently keeping their inclinations veiled. Most of them are keen that 'no-one should notice anything'. I know homosexuals in Berlin, even a few who are not at all abstemious, who have managed to fool those around them for years, decades, their whole lives even; it is also common for them to transform a male character into a female when reporting romantic adventures to their companions, just as some translators of the writers of antiquity do.

The physical configuration of Berlin is a great boon in this transformation. Anyone living in the east who conducts his business and family relations there can meet up with friends in the south for years without those in his circle being any the wiser. There are many Berliners in the west who have never seen Wedding, many in Kreuzberg who have never stepped foot in the Scheunenviertel[6]. For a long time I have treated an old Berlin lady, the widow of a musician. She had one child, a son, who had set off on the wrong path, playing truant from an early age, disappearing for days on end and roaming about. His parents would always go looking for him but when he turned 21 they lost their patience, and let him go. For 26 years the mother had neither seen nor heard from her boy; she was over 70, her husband long dead. And then one day he simply reappeared, a prematurely aged 47-year-old man with a shaggy beard, a vagrant with an 'organism poisoned by alcohol'; he wanted to know if she perhaps 'still had some of Father's old clothes'. The most unusual thing – in those 26 years neither mother nor son had left Berlin. Such a case would never occur in a small town.

It beggars imagination how many can elude the authorities entirely in the Prussian capital, which is seen as a model of order, a status it may rightfully claim when set against other major cities. I have been astonished to witness foreigners remaining unhindered in Berlin long after they were officially expelled, more astonished still to see how those sought by the police can stay here for months and years without registering with the authorities, and not even in outlying districts, but usually near the great transport junctions where their presence would be least suspected.

Have you ever been to Room 361 of the police headquarters on Alexanderplatz[7]? It is one of the most remarkable places in a city scarcely wanting for striking locations. Perched high above the roofs of the metropolis, it is to be found in the middle of a row of rooms in which ten million pieces of paper are arranged in alphabetical order. Each sheet represents a human life. Those among the living are found in the blue cartons, the dead repose in white. Each sheet bears the name, place of birth and date of birth of each person who has inhabited an apartment or room in Berlin since the year 1836. Every registration and deregistration, every change of address is scrupulously recorded. There are sheets that contain thirty or more apartments, others with only one; there are those whose lifespans begin in a cellar in the east and stretch all the way to the Tiergarten district[8], and others who start off on the first floor of the front block of the building and end their days on the fourth floor of a rear block[9]. Anyone seeking to find a missing person in Berlin is directed to Room 361. From eight o'clock in the morning to seven o'clock at night, they climb the steep stone steps in their hundreds, many thousands over the course of a year. Each piece of information costs 25 pfennigs. These are not just people seeking to recover money, those who value others purely by the debt they represent. No, many of those mounting the stairs have returned from distant lands and are now trying to determine where (or if) their close relations and childhood friends now live. For the first few years they continued to write to each other, then their correspondence abated, and now the stranger has once more returned to the old homeland. Hearts racing, they write their mother's name and last known abode on the information slip – but she is long dead; they ask after brothers, sisters and friends, all of them, every one of them dead, and with heavy heart the lonely supplicant descends the stairs once more.

How many enquire there, fruitlessly, parents seeking prodigal sons, sisters enquiring after brothers, and girls looking for the fathers of the children whose futures lie in their wombs. 'Not registered', 'forwarding address unknown', 'emigrated', 'dead' report the officials, always dispassionate, when they return after half an hour and summon the waiting applicant, who then silently, gravely, despondently, all too rarely joyfully, goes back down the stairs to be consumed once more by the tide of buildings and people in this formidable city, Berlin.

The ease with which one can sink unseen into a city of two and a half million inhabitants greatly facilitates the dual personality so often found in the sexual arena. The professional self and the sexual self, day self and night self are often two utterly distinct personalities in one body, the one proud and honourable, most noble and conscientious, the other its antithesis. This applies to homosexuals as well as the normally sexed. I knew a uranian lawyer who, on leaving his office near Potsdamer Platz of an evening, or taking leave of a gathering of his associates, would seek out a tavern at the southern end of Friedrichstadt[10], a dive bar where he would gamble, drink and carouse the night away with 'Revolver Heini', 'Butcher Herrmann', 'Yankee Franzi', 'Mad Dog'[11] and other Berlin apaches[12]. The raw nature of these criminals seemed to exert an irresistible attraction. Another, a former officer from one of the foremost families in the country, went further still. Two or three evenings a week he would swap his dress coat for an old jacket, his top hat for a flat cap, his high collar for a colourful kerchief, donning a sweater, boatman's trousers and army boots and whiling away a few hours in the bars of the Scheunenviertel, whose inhabitants imagined him to be one of their own. At four o'clock in the morning he would make his way to the 'Hammelstall', a pub near

Friedrichstrasse station popular with the unemployed[13], eat a 10-pfennig breakfast with the poorest vagabonds, and after a few hours' sleep awaken once more to his existence as an irreproachable gentleman.

I also remember a homosexual lady who lived a very similar double life, a cook who sought out dance halls frequented by servants, in whose midst she felt particularly at ease.

This splitting or – if you will – doubling of the personality is particularly noteworthy in those situations where it is additionally associated with a division into two sexes.

I have in my possession a photograph of a man dressed as an elegant lady, a man who for many years was a fixture among the women of the Parisian demi-monde, until by accident it was revealed that 'she' was, in fact, a man, and not even a homosexual. In Berlin, too, men have repeatedly been picked up serving as female prostitutes. There is more than one woman in Berlin who is known to live entirely as a man at home. I encountered one such during a function at the Philharmonic, where her deep voice and manly gait seized my attention. I made her acquaintance and asked if I might call upon her. The next Sunday afternoon around dusk I rang her doorbell; a young man answered, attended by an excitable dog – the man had a lit cigar in his hand and asked what my business was. 'I wish to speak with Miss X., could you please give her my card.' 'Step a little closer,' answered the young lad with a laugh, 'it is I.' I discovered that this maiden lived her domestic life completely as a man, a doughty individual who had bravely joined battle with life and rejected many a proposal of marriage which would have seen her 'taken care of' because she did not want to 'deceive a man'.

This split in personality can extend so far that the daylight soul is filled with moral indignation at the nocturnal self, combatting it assiduously. It is not always simple hypocrisy at work when one who is known to lash out scornfully at the homosexual one day falls afoul of Paragraph 175[14] of the Criminal Code.

And so if a large number of uranians – and this is undoubtedly the case – choose to live chastely even in Berlin, where sexual intercourse is relatively easy and safe, this is apt to spring not so much from concern but rather because some other character trait compels and enables chastity. Many of these homosexuals live as bachelors, completely alone; some can only still their sexual urges through intensive mental exertion, others might appear eccentric, and indeed often have something crotchety, spinsterish about them, others develop a great enthusiasm for collecting, which often involves objects related in some way to their inclinations. I know of one uranian prince in Berlin, for instance, with a true passion for collecting depictions of soldiers of every era and nation. Others aim to channel and satisfy their sexual urges by seeking out those places – swimming pools, gymnasiums, sports grounds – which afford them the enjoyable sight of pleasing figures, or finally they may themselves establish such an organisation. Among the single-sex organisations of Berlin – the gymnastics clubs, young men's Christian associations[15], as well as women's clubs and organisations from servants' associations to suffrage leagues – there are often uranian members; in fact the uranian element is not infrequently the driving force of the association. These uranian individuals are often only dimly conscious of their own inclinations, if at all, and might only become aware when a third party, usually more in jest than earnest, makes an observation like, 'you carry on like a sissy'[16].

Some time ago a member of a spiritualist association called on me so I might confirm whether he was homosexual or not; during an argument, a fellow member shouted at him, 'shut up hermaphrodite'. This very feminine and clearly highly strung youth reported that he had no sensual impulses toward either women or men in his day-to-day life, and only when he fell into a trance state, which came to him easily, did he believe himself to be an Indian lady who experienced strong romantic feelings toward one of his fellow members.

While uranians usually know to control themselves in their associations, now and then there is a 'scandal' when a dash of alcohol loosens the reins with which they ordinarily keep their true natures under control. Here I table an example which is instructive from numerous perspectives.

Around ten years ago a missionary in a house dedicated to religious works would stage large gatherings and festivities which were particularly well attended. 'The winsome, amiable nature of this man drew them like a magnet.' He was a person of the most distinguished appearance, in his mid-thirties, highly talented and a splendid conversationalist. 'He had only to ask, and the donations would pour in; in all arenas he was authoritative, beloved and admired, particularly among the womenfolk.' Words could not express the goodness of his heart; in these gatherings he himself would often report how he administered succour in the prisons, frequently and willingly, how he would find young people in institutions without a penny to their names, take them back to the house and let them stay. And all this with a cheerful demeanour all the while. Anyone who observed him during the association's summer excursions, staging competitions with his pupils, wrestling with them, playing so boisterously, would delight in the apparently harmless joy of this tireless soldier for God without suspecting a thing. One day, however, the pious establishment was cast into deep sorrow and great indignation. Mister W. had been arrested for immoral deeds with young men. During the court case twelve youths reported that W. had touched them indecently, even behind the pulpit, at the organ and in the sacristy, always joining them in prayer afterwards. He received a heavy prison sentence.

This report came to me from a very honourable uranian who belonged to the same Christian organisation. 'I would never,' he wrote to me, 'have believed that this respectable man could fall so suddenly from such a height, that my inner sentiments, which I struggled to suppress, and for the intended mastery of which I had sought out that pious society, would also be shared by that society's leader. As the tragedy I describe unfolded, the humble thought came to me: "Lord, forgive this sinner", and like many others I left that sorely damaged association.'

The platonic homosexual often dedicates himself not so much to an association as to a single individual who takes his fancy. How many of these men allow their protégés to learn and study, taking them travelling, providing them with an income, adopting them, remembering them in their wills, caring for them in the most intensive way, without so much as a kiss coming between them, without the party in question even being aware of the sexual foundation of this proclivity, although he awaits letters from his friend with no less longing, reads them no less avidly than a groom those of his bride. And even less frequently is the receiving party in such relationships aware of the true nature of his 'paternal' friend. He and his family may well be full of praise for 'the good heart' of their best friend, but that does not prevent the young man from thoroughly badmouthing homosexuals from time to time, never suspecting how much it affects the one he would least wish to injure.

Here I wish to bring to the reader's attention a poem by a Berlin uranian dedicated to his friend[17], which vividly illustrates the difficulty of defining those imperceptibly merging lines between the intellectual, spiritual and physical expression of sentiment which may differ in form and intensity, but not in essence. It reads:

> To gaze into those deep and trusting eyes,
> And standing at my window side by side,
> My face and his now pressing cheek to cheek,
> So close, so long, we barely dare to speak
> Is that not joy enough
> To touch his hand, to feel his soft caress,

To feel, to hear the breath rise in his chest,
To lean my head down soft upon his heart
And press my mouth to his, our lips apart,
Yes, that is joy enough

His joy is mine, I long to hear him laugh
Yet even grave and still, my other half
Is always different, and yet the same
His strength and beauty are ever aflame
Is that not joy enough

To speak with him, to share what pains our hearts,
His voice a ringing bell, a singing harp,
To make his journey sweeter and to lay
My hand on his to soothe the pain away
Yes, that is joy enough

His love for me that lifts me high above,
And mine for him, there is no greater love,
To show him how I love him, yes and then,
To hear his wish that I remain his friend,
Yes, that is joy enough

Would that I had known that I would never
Find a greater joy, so why endeavour
To search for more than that which is my due,
The peace I find is great enough for two
To both have joy enough.

The following detailed report from a chaste uranian on
the first awakening of love – originating from a student

of my acquaintance who has never been sexually active – serves also to confirm that the homosexual drive may differ from normally sexed love in its orientation and meaning, but not in natural vitality.

I grew up in the 'Babylon' of Berlin, attended a public school with many fellow students of the same age; I even boarded there, which was fairly rough and tumble, and I remained curiously childish, especially when it came to sexual relationships. Unlike other children I never took pleasure in discussing and pondering 'where children come from', I even felt a strange reticence in talking about such things, the origin of which is still unclear to me. So at 15 years of age my classmates regarded me, and not without cause, as 'innocent'. While I no longer believed in the stork, I was ignorant as to the nature of the difference between the sexes and of any type of sexual relationship. Naturally I understood nothing of the widespread jokes around these topics, a fact that served to confirm my reputation as an innocent.

Around this time, when I was 17 years old, I developed an unusual affection for one of my classmates, the head of the class. I was not as close to him as I was to my special school friends, but I always experienced a particular joy when I had the opportunity of speaking to him at length, walking through the schoolyard with him, or even sitting next to him in lessons. To my dismay this was something I only rarely managed, I was almost always the third so that there was someone else between us, and I had to be satisfied with looking at him as often as possible, although I was careful that he should not observe me doing so. And I took the utmost pains that others should notice nothing of my relations with him which, by the way, were and remain one-sided. Then as now I can offer no good reason why I should keep my fondness a secret, particularly from the object of my affections. I probably thought, quite rightly, that I would encounter incomprehension, and even I had only a dim understanding of my situation and would never have been able to express it, to say in words what I actually thought and felt back then. But it was so heavenly to imagine what it would be like if we really were friends, if we were always together, doing our homework together, never having to part. And when I lay in bed at night, I imagined all the possible scenarios that might transpire for us to become true friends. His house might burn down, for instance, he would have nowhere to live and I would take him in to live with us; and then he would even sleep in my bed, so I could hold him tight and press against him, to show him how much I loved him.

Yes, these thoughts would come to me and fill me with untold bliss although I had no idea about sexual relationships. My mind was completely pure, unspoilt by smutty, dirty stories, the kind that other children of the metropolis often hear all too early; my imagination was not roused by such things. So why was I visited by these 'immoral, indecent' imaginings? No, there was nothing the least bit immoral in these thoughts, it could not be that, and these certainties, which I have experienced in myself, which I have felt and thought from the bottom of my heart, are the surest and most irrevocable proof that homosexuality in itself has not the faintest trace of that which ignorance and unknowing ascribe to it. Unless one sees the sexual as something inherently immoral, unless one seeks to offend the natural order of the world by dragging that which is most holy in people's lives through the muck, then you might very well condemn same-sex love along with it. Now I know that what I experienced back then was nothing other than the first awakening of love in a mind still child-like, with no idea of what it was experiencing, but which was nonetheless filled with this fresh glory.

And just as the first object of my affections was male, so it has remained for me until now. When other 'normal' men on the street see a pretty girl, they reflexively turn their heads; for me it is exactly the same with handsome youths – my attention is just as reflexive. If I arrive at a gathering, a ball or such, it often happens that, quite unbidden, I notice one of the young people yet unknown to me and later I realise that I have been constantly watching what he is doing, who he dances with, and so on.

After some time that first love was replaced by another, greater passion which drew me to a different school companion, who was a whole year older than I, but nonetheless a class below me.

I still remember how the first signs of this love gradually arose in me, how I took advantage of every opportunity to be with him – in the playground, on the street, during gymnastics, and so on. And yet it was particularly difficult to maintain this contact; not only because he was in another class, but also because we really did not have any shared interests, or mutual friends, in fact he was decidedly unpopular among my circle of friends. So it must have been all the more conspicuous when I drew closer to him and used the most varied reasons to justify this closeness, not just to others but to myself as well, because I still did not know what I was experiencing. But it was precisely around this time, when I was 18 years old, that the true nature of things dawned on me, this at a time when I would regularly stroll past his house, calculating the time when he would emerge so I could 'accidentally' bump into him, and thought of nothing but him. Yes, I soon realised that I really, truly loved him, but I never had the courage to tell him and for a long time even took pains to prevent him noticing it. We saw each other ever more frequently, although I knew that he did not think all that much of me; I used every opportunity to make our relationship closer and more friendly, which succeeded at least for appearances, but despite my greatest efforts it never really developed into a close friendship. It was in K.'s nature not to have friends, and so in this period I was only once forced to encounter the agony of jealousy; but it was precisely this fit of jealousy, which truly upset me, that also made the nature of my homosexual love completely clear. So overwhelming were the feelings that drew me to him, so weary was I of pretending to him and to myself, that finally one evening as we were working in his room I hugged him and showered him with kisses and confessed all. He was surprised by this outburst, but took it quite calmly without ever truly comprehending what it all meant.

There followed the greatest weeks of my life to date; we were together almost every evening, I would help him with all his schoolwork, and when we were finished, we would sit pressed against each other, talking about everything and nothing. But sadly this only lasted a few weeks, for it was exactly around this time that K. became aware of his love – not for me, but rather some girl. And when I went to see him in the afternoon, he would talk of nothing but her, and on the way to school he would talk to me about her, and in the evening I would go along with him when he met her, and I would wait until she came, exchange a few words with her, walk a little way with them and then take my leave and let them alone, my presence now superfluous. I could not say that I was jealous, exactly. On the contrary, part of my love for K. spilled over to his girlfriend, because she was the one who made him happy. But my heart bled nonetheless, when he showed me his diary, for example, in which there was nothing but her, what she did and said and thought, and barely a mention of me. What pained me most of all, however, was that he vehemently refused to accept my kisses and caresses; precisely because I had made it clear to him that my feelings for him were true love, because I had convinced him with all the means at my disposal that my love for him was justified, just like the love between man and woman, for this very reason he claimed that it would be an infidelity to her if he let me go on kissing him. 'We can still be friends,' he said, 'because I really like you, but we can only be as other friends.'

And so we remained friends for another two years, and I flatter myself that early on at least I exerted a truly positive influence on him; not only by helping him with his work, but also trying to instil more elevated interests than he sadly otherwise held, to awaken in him a consideration for issues of science, and politics, and so forth, which the education he received, the milieu in which he lived and his own indifference had hitherto failed to rouse. My love for him retained its intensity over a long period, and even today I have yet to completely recover from this passion.

As the years went by I gradually began to notice my predisposition, at first only in a negative sense. When my schoolmates started talking about their loved ones, whose names they would scratch into the school bench, to whom they sent postcards at every opportunity, at first I fancied that I too would feel like that one day, especially as I was always one of the youngest in the class. And at the same time I failed to realise that my affection for K. was nothing other than real, genuine love, perhaps stronger and deeper than most of the others felt for their girlfriends. It was only through analogous examples that happened to arise that the true nature of things became apparent to me. Like any true lover I paraded before his window, went past his house daily, as often as possible, even when it required the greatest detour, and was always happy to see him standing at the window. And so it dawned on me and, conscious of it now and seeking other indications, I became halfway aware of myself. I well remember, for example, the deep impression it made on me when his mother said to me in jest one day: 'Paul, Paul, anyone who walks around by himself like you do must be in love'; indeed I never took my brother along purely because if I encountered him, I wanted to be alone with him.

'Steady relationships' between homosexual men and women, often of significant duration, are extraordinarily common in Berlin.

It is something you have to experience – the numerous unmistakable examples of the tenderness, the bonds that so often unite one with the other, how they care for one another and long for one another, how the lover empathises with the loved one's interests, often so far from his own, the scholar in the affairs of the worker, the artist in those of the sergeant; you have to witness the tortures of body and soul with which these people not infrequently suffer jealousy, and only then does it become apparent that this is not a 'case of unnatural fornication'[18], but rather a part of that great sensation that many believe lends human existence its value, its consecration.

I used to treat an aristocratic lady who had lived with a female friend for a number of years and suffered from a serious nervous complaint. Neither before nor after in my medical practice have I ever seen such loving devotion of a healthy person toward an invalid as in this case, not between spouses, nor in mothers fretting for their children. The healthy friend was hardly an agreeable individual, there was much that was inconsiderate and obstinate about her, but anyone who witnessed this truly touching love and care, this ceaseless effort day and night, would have credited it to strong, fine sentiment. It was as though the two were joined at the hip. Touch the pained limb of the invalid and the other would flinch reflexively, any discomfort of the patient was reflected in her face, insomnia and poor appetite transferred to the healthy friend. The case was also noteworthy for the fact that the patient's staff, both the nurse and the maid, were unimpeachably uranian.

Not far from this couple lived another, a trainee lawyer and his friend of around 18 years of age, who was a dressmaker. The latter was so feminine that the lawyer once observed that he could just as well have fallen in love with a real woman as this nine-tenths of a woman. His voice, for example, was so womanly that whenever he telephoned and asked to speak to me, my secretary would invariably say, 'a lady wishes to speak with you'. The two lived in perfect harmony, each went to his own work every day, the one to the court, the other to the dressmakers'. When the lawyer left Berlin, he took his friend with him. When his father, a simple Berlin labourer, asked him to explain, he – as he related with shame – had to dim the light in the room. It came as no surprise to the father, who had long suspected something of the sort, and he declared himself in agreement with the situation.

The little dressmaker had a colleague, no less girlish than he. Their profession is more apt to attract the uranian element than any other in Berlin. This colleague fell in love with the lawyer's brother, an engineer, who shortly before had undertaken a serious attempt at suicide following an unhappy affair with a male student. As he lay seriously injured in hospital, he and his similarly oriented brother revealed all, neither having previously suspected the other. Gradually a second love pact developed between the engineer and the other dressmaker, and there was no little drollery when the two handsome, well-built brothers strolled through the Grunewald[19] of a Sunday with their two little dressmaker boys Willi and Hans, just like the others parading with their milliner sweethearts.

In Berlin it is far from unheard of for parents to come to an accommodation with the uranian natures, even the homosexual lives, of their children.

Recently I attended the burial of an old doctor in a cemetery on the outskirts of Berlin. At the open grave stood the only son of the deceased, to the right the aged mother, on the other side the 20-year-old friend, all three in deepest mourning. The father was over 70 years old when he became aware of his son's uranian nature and, close to despair, he sought out several alienists who could offer advice but no assistance. Then he immersed himself in literature on the topic and increasingly came to recognise that his son, whom he loved more than anything, had been homosexual from birth. At his residence, he had no objection to the son taking in his friend, indeed the good parents transferred all their love to the young man, who came from the most humble background. They exerted an obvious positive influence on each other; while each would have had difficulty getting ahead on his own, as a pair they managed splendidly, because the wisdom and kindness of the one found its complement in the energy and thrift of the other.

On his deathbed the old doctor bade farewell to his wife and his 'two lads', and the sight of these three individuals, united in tears and mourning to the sound of Mendelssohn's 'It Is Surely God's Will'[20], made a much deeper impression on the soul than the eulogy of the shrill young priest, praising the deeds of the deceased to whom he was a complete stranger.

In Berlin it is not unusual to find uranian bachelors moving in with their friends' families, where they are treated like any other member of the household. There are mothers, often well aware of the circumstances, who exuberantly, happily relate that their son, their daughter has found such a wonderful friend; that these friendships are preferable by far to their sons messing about with girls, or their daughters being courted by men. One mother, who had sought me out because her son had acquired a venereal disease, went so far as to say, 'I wish my other son were homosexual as well'. Sometimes the friend loves the son of the house and is loved in turn by the daughter; peculiar entanglements arise among the assortment of normally sexed and homosexual, much as they do everywhere. To the psychologist and writer able to recognise the uranian motive in human relationships, this spreads conflict in unforeseen ways that merit observation and description.

I knew a uranian in Berlin who married the sister of a youth solely that he might be together – often and inconspicuously – with the brother. The marriage, which in fact was nothing of the sort, fell apart after a few years when the normally sexed brother relieved his brother-in-law of a considerable sum of money, albeit through honest means.

Another homosexual loved a man who had forged a deep emotional bond with a girl. The uranian was highly jealous of the girl, who herself did not have a good word to say about the friend who monopolised so much of her beloved's time. However, the man was unfaithful to the girl and caused her, as well as the friend, much pain with his careless antics. The two did not know each other personally. But one morning the girl went to the uranian to inform him that his friend had suffered a serious accident during the night. Their mutual concern gradually transformed into friendship. Then the man and the girl split up. She was furious and apparently inconsolable, he could not fight his desire, was drawn back to her, but she showed him the door. Finally he turned to his uranian friend and begged for help and he, who had silently rejoiced that the affair that had caused him such torment was at an end, went to the girl and reunited the two.

I could relate numerous identical or similar cases from the vibrant wellspring of Berlin life – but at this point we should shift our focus from the lives and laments of uranian individuals to the lives and activities of uranian groups.

Because while many uranians do indeed live their lives in self-imposed solitude, which is easier to achieve in the amplitude of the metropolis than anywhere else, and others dedicate themselves solely to another, there is no lack of those who seek contact with homosexual individuals and groupings, and here too Berlin boasts a great wealth of opportunities.

It is truly regrettable that so many uranians, whose nature and knowledge would enrich any group, feel uncomfortable in normal associations. The feigned compliments and interests, the 'toast to the ladies' frequently directed at them become ever more embarrassing, and when they discover true conviviality in which they can give freely of themselves and find understanding, they withdraw more and more from other circles.

Gregarious groupings of uranians prosper in highly diverse forms and with exceptional vivacity in Berlin, both in closed as well as generally accessible circles. Variously sized gatherings of homosexuals, for homosexuals, can be experienced throughout the year, particularly in winter.

Many of these are restricted to a certain social stratum, to particular classes and stations in life, but these barriers are not nearly as strictly observed as they are among the normally sexed, for the sake of the respective friends if nothing else. Many uranians could imagine nothing more offensive than a friend, no matter how humble his background, being denied equality in company.

In acknowledgment of my work for the liberation of homosexuals I am often asked to attend such events as a guest of honour, and even though I can only accept a small number of these invitations, they have been sufficient to provide me with an insight into the social life of the Berlin uranian.

In said capacity I once found myself in a gathering of obviously homosexual princes, counts and barons. Apart from the servants who, while not great in number seemed nonetheless to have been carefully chosen for their appearances, there was little to distinguish this event from any such gathering of gentlemen of their class. As they sat at small tables eating fine foods, lively discussion broke out about the latest productions of Wagner, for whom educated uranians, almost without exception, evince a strong affinity[21]. The talk then turned to travel and literature, skirting politics almost entirely, before gradually arriving at court gossip. They dwelt in detail on the latest court ball, where the appearance of the young Duke of X. set many a uranian heart aflutter; they swooned over his blue uniform, his captivating manners and discussed how one might secure an introduction to His Royal Highness. Then came anecdotes about uranians from court society not present at the gathering, of which one, greeted with particularly fulsome laughter, has stuck in my memory. A prince had been invited to a hunt party by a homosexual magnate[22], of whose uranian nature he was as ignorant as those of other men of his acquaintance. The esteemed guest rose unexpectedly early to stroll around the palace garden. Traversing the corridor he caught sight of his host, ill-prepared for an encounter at such an early hour, in a highly unusual costume, or rather get-up; this country squire, quite rounded on all sides, was wearing a red satin matinée jacket embroidered with flowers and lace. The sight of this garb was so comic that the princely visitor was overcome by an actual fit of laughter.

Another event that I attended took place in the reception rooms of one of Berlin's most prestigious hotels. A wealthy uranian was celebrating his name day. The event's attendees were, with few exceptions, male couples, most of whom had already been cohabiting for some years; each sat at the table with his 'love'. The feast in the side hall was preceded by a theatrical presentation offered solely by homosexuals on a stage set up for the purpose. After a few solo routines the masked host played Falstaff in a scene from the *Merry Wives of Windsor*, then came Nestroy's Viennese farce *A Lecture at the Housmistress's*[23]. The female roles, of which there was no lack in this piece, were all played by feminine uranians, with one well-known baron attracting wild applause for his naturalistic performance in the title role. After the dinner came dancing, and although the wine flowed freely, nothing indecent transpired. With some guests already in women's clothing, a few dared the harmless lark of fitting the particularly masculine uranians with hats and scarves and other items of female clothing; some took this wicked jest with alacrity, but others were vexed. There are uranians who are so averse to women and all things feminine that the idea that they themselves might exhibit womanly traits is intolerable.

In less prosperous uranian circles, as well, there are popular and widespread gatherings in Berlin. Here too I can recall an example. One homosexual who had experienced few of the good things in life was celebrating his birthday. The party took place in a small tavern on the outskirts and among the invitees were his two normally sexed brothers. All partook heartily of the sausages, potato salad and Swiss cheese, while the publican's son bashed out popular songs on the piano. Then came a performance by 'Schwanhilde', also known as 'Mister Swan née Hilde', a noted Berlin uranian. He played a female Berlin cook who was drawn to the stage, and was particularly amusing at the close when he parodied the barefoot dancer Isadora Duncan[24]. A female impersonator of the lowest order, who happened to be sitting in the front room of the establishment, was asked to present his repertoire. In between these acts appeared a real man, a coal trader from the Landwehr Canal[25], a 'hard lad' with tattooed arms, shaved head, woollen jumper and that strange amalgam of grace und ungainliness that is the hallmark of his type. He sang a whole suite of not entirely decent songs in the Berliner style, with not a trace of a voice, numerous grammatical errors, each line accompanied by grotesque gestures, verses bookended by twirls, everything about his clumsiness somehow so apt that it was not without effect. Gradually the tables and chairs were pushed to one side and the dancing began, including one episode of a humour difficult to relate. With the dancing in full swing – this, mind, being long past closing time – there suddenly appeared a policeman with a stern, officious demeanour. The cheerful mood was interrupted for only a moment when one of the guests – a uranian musician – grabbed the officer by the waist and waltzed him hence. He was so shocked that he could scarcely offer resistance, eagerly joining in the dance and soon vying with the publican's son and the coal carrier for the role of most desired and sought-after dance partner.

Naturally there are also many uranian events that are far more serious in nature. There was a private scholar who would host a small circle in his artistically decorated home several times each winter. The attendees usually comprised ten to twelve gentlemen from academic circles, all but two or three of them homosexual. The old man, who treated his guests to heavy fortified wines, oysters, lobster and similar delicacies, had even known Alexander von Humboldt and Iffland[26] in his time, had been a friend of Hermann Hendrichs[27] and Karl Ulrichs, and seemed inexhaustible in his reminiscences. These talks were almost solely preoccupied with the homosexual problem. A young Catholic religious debated with a grey-haired Evangelical priest about uranianism and Christianity: a number of philologists clashed over Shakespeare's sonnets, while the lawyers and doctors discussed the extent to which Paragraph 51[28] of the Criminal Code, which covered exclusions to the exercise of free will, might even then be used to the advantage of homosexuals.

Gravest of all the gatherings attended by Berlin's uranians are those staged on Christmas Eve. It is on this more than any other day, this feast of familial joy, that the uranian bachelor feels the burden of his solitary fate. Many would find the evening even sadder were it not for the wealthier homosexuals, one or the other of whom always plays host to waifs and strays.

Here again I draw on an example from the metropolis.

Days before the holiday the master of the house himself decorates the Christmas tree, a large silver fir; nothing too colourful, rather silver garlands entwined around white candles, icicles, snowflakes, glass globes and angel's hair, draped from branch to branch like spiders' webs, all in the best taste. And high on the treetop a large silver star, on which a trumpeting angel in a light tulle gown proclaims 'peace on Earth to all men'. Then the little presents are meticulously wrapped in tissue paper and laid about the tree, something for everyone – a calendar, a book, a little trinket, or even a chain ring, a hand mirror, a moustache trainer. In the early hours of the 24th the master of the house fetches the tablecloth of finest linen from the cupboard, and the servants dress the table, lay out the silver, fold the napkins, fill the hefty fruit bowl, decorate each plate with a posy and lay delicate table cards before the crystal glasses. But difficulties may arise when trying to recall the real names of some of the guests. All year round one answers solely to a nickname, but it is a name one is keen to distance oneself from this evening.

A second table is set up in the corridor, there the children and the servants have their Christmas dinner – yes indeed, children, a rare sight in uranian homes. The washing lady's two small children and the concierge's three grandchildren are invited in as the gifts are handed out. It is a point of honour that the same meals are brought to both the main table and this side table, and that here too everything should look particularly festive.

The start is set for 8 o'clock, because a few attendees are in the habit of exchanging gifts at the homes of family members or companions before they come to this circle of friends. Finally, with everyone present, the master of the house disappears into the drawing room which has been closed until now, lights the candles, casts a final glance over the presents and calls in the children and a guest who accompanies their Christmas carols at the piano. Now the double doors are opened to the children's bright tones singing of quiet, holy nights and blessed, joyful Christmastime[29].

There is an expression of great gravity on every face, a tear clouds the odd eye, even the ladies' dressmaker 'Lanky Emily', usually so amusing, is overcome by his emotions. Far, far back wander the thoughts of the uranians at such moments, to the time when this day was also a family celebration, when there was nothing yet to indicate a fate so different from that of their long-wed siblings; only gradually did that cleft which divided them from others open, then came the long years when they would spend this eve friendless and joyless in a restaurant or with 'a good book' in their 'furnished room'. Many think about their shattered hopes, what they could have achieved if old prejudices had not hindered their progress, and others in respectable positions ponder the heavy lie they must live. Many think about their parents who are dead – or for whom they are dead – and all in deepest sorrow think of the woman they loved most of all and who loved them most of all – their mother.

The children's voices now fallen quiet, the little gifts are exchanged, children and servants being particularly well catered for, and all take their places. The table talk flows less freely than usual; there is discussion of the good X. who attended last year's Christmas Eve and now lies in the ground.

Slowly the tension eases, the tone lightens a little, but the grave undertone remains, and a veil of sentimental weltschmerz lays over the entire evening.

'Praise God in the highest and peace on Earth to all men! When, then,' – as one homosexual wrote to me some years ago on Christmas Eve – 'when will people finally acknowledge that the Saviour came unto us too, that we should not be cast out from his gracious, noble, merciful, all-embracing love?'

It was early last Christmas morning when I was called to the home of a uranian student in western Berlin who had apparently had a fit of apoplexy the previous evening.

An appalling sight awaited me on my arrival; the entire room was filled with scraps and pieces of furniture, torn cloths, books and papers, all of it doused with blood, ink and petroleum. There was a large pool of blood by the bed, and there lay a young man whose deathly pale face was pierced by flaming eyes of an unusual depth, black wisps of hair surrounding his fine, regular features. His forehead and arms were wrapped in blood-soaked cloths.

His uranianism had caused him to fall out with his strict father, a respected citizen of Berlin, and neither had a good word to say for the other and now, far from his family home, he had spent Christmas Eve wandering aimlessly about the empty streets of the metropolis. From the other side of the street, crouching in a dark passageway, he had observed the glowing lights in his parents' apartment, the laughter of his younger siblings reaching his ears and for a few moments he saw the silhouette of his mother who pressed her forehead to the window pane, deep in thought, while the children played.

As the lights went out above, he went to the nearest bar and downed one schnapps after another at a secluded corner table, repeated the procedure in a second and third tavern and spent the last of his money on black coffee and kirsch in desolate cafés.

Returning home in the cold winter night and unsteadily mounting the four flights in the rear block, he was seized by a wild frenzy. He wrecked everything and shattered the burning lamp in the expectation that he would bleed to death from his severed arteries. A doctor who had quickly been summoned by the housemaster peeked through the crack in the door and hastily wrote out a certificate for transfer to the mental department of the Charité[30].

A friend of the patient brought me to him; I washed and bandaged one wound after the other on that Christmas morning; he made no complaint, said nothing at all, but his flaming eyes, his pale lips, every one of his wounds – they all spoke of a deep suffering and the high, holy work of those who strive to liberate the uranian.

Along with the private gatherings, dinners, suppers, coffee circles, afternoon teas, picnics, house balls and summer parties, of which more than a few are staged by Berlin homosexuals, here it is particularly worth mentioning the *jours fixes* that a few uranian men and women stage for their male and female friends.

For a number of years a particularly renowned Sunday afternoon reception took place at the home of a uranian chamberlain, attracting many persons of rank and status. For bodily needs there were tea and pastries, spiritual nourishment came in the form of musical presentations.

Last winter the *jour fixe* of one uranian artist was especially popular. This highly hospitable host received his guests – who included numerous homosexual foreigners, particularly those from the Russian Baltic provinces and Scandinavian countries, and a number of homosexual ladies – in an intermediary[31] vesture, a cross between a princess's dress and ceremonial robe.

The musical presentations, especially the host's baritone and alto and the Danish pianist, were of the highest artistic standard. An Austrian chemistry student was regularly seen there, always silent and solemn, although his recurring visits suggested that he felt comfortable there among his own kind. In spring, when the gatherings came to an end and the Russian departed Berlin, this student went to a uranian tavern one evening and had the pianist play Koschat's 'Forsaken'[32]; as the melancholy air came to an end, no one noticed him taking a small piece of cyanide, which within a few seconds lay him prostrate on the floor. 'Suicide for reasons unknown,' read the police report; in fact it was the suicide of a homosexual, something that occurs all too often in Berlin.

Homosexuality is not always the direct cause, but one can almost always establish an indirect link between homosexuality and the violent end. There was the uranian officer, raised in the cadet corps, a soldier through and through, who disgraced himself with an off-duty homosexual encounter; it came to light and he was forced to depart discreetly. He had learnt nothing but the art of war, he tried to find employment as a merchant, sought, found and lost one lover after another. His family wanted nothing to do with him, he stood alone, he lost his footing, sank ever deeper, he reached for alcohol, for morphine and ultimately for the redemption of the revolver.

One among the many tragedies I am aware of; just a few weeks ago a former lieutenant met a similar end. 'Cause of death: debt,' wrote the newspapers. Debt, true enough, but the real cause lay deeper, in a development similar to the one I recount above – it was homosexuality that caused his downfall.

Some days ago I took a flask of prussic acid

from a homosexual teacher who had come to see me. He had committed no criminal offence, had never indulged in same-sex activities; he had just started working at a school when the principal received an anonymous letter claiming the new teacher to be a pederast[33]. The principal summoned him and upon questioning he admitted his homosexual inclinations. The principal, meaning well, advised him to tender his resignation, which he did, but he lacked the courage to tell his aged mother who had lived in penury so that he might become a teacher. Now he wandered about in search of a position in our great city of Berlin, where there are so many jobs, but so many more jobless.

Over the last eight years I have managed to save at least twenty homosexuals from suicide; whether I did them a good turn I do not know, and yet it fills me with a silent joy that I was able save their lives.

Similar to these *jours fixes*, and perhaps even more club-like in tone, are the regular gatherings held by homosexuals on certain evenings in certain bars; here, too, it is usually one figure around whom the others gravitate, but all serve themselves with their own means. The 'Lohengrin' club, held at the establishment of a wine merchant known as 'The Queen', was popular for some years. While the entertainment there consisted of musical and oratorical offerings, many of these associations, such as the 'Community of the Self'[34] and the 'Platen Community'[35] are more literary in nature. There is also a cabaret in Berlin which is run and primarily patronised by uranians.

At all of these events, sexuality as such recedes

into the background just as it does in corresponding circles of the normally sexed. The element that binds the community together is simply a feeling of belonging arising from a commonality of destiny.

While the above-named societies tend to be closed in nature, there are a great many more that are widely accessible. That many restaurants, hotels, pensions, bathing facilities and pleasure spots are, although open to all, almost exclusively patronised by uranians, appears less unusual when you consider how many less clearly defined groups in Berlin have their localities that derive their existence almost entirely from that group. There are restaurants patronised solely by students, by actors, by artists, others that survive purely from merchants of certain wares, adherents of particular games and sports, and still others that are frequented exclusively by bookmakers, cardsharps and other categories of criminal.

One may draw a distinction between those localities preferred by uranians yet still patronised by others, and those exclusively patronised by them. Among the former is a very large Munich beer hall in Friedrichstadt, where for years there have been around a hundred homosexuals, sometimes more, at certain times. And uranians prefer certain cafés, although this changes every few years; often these are locations where the landlord or a waiter himself is uranian, and in most cases there are certain areas of the premises that are particularly favoured.

Many uranian ladies meet in patisseries; in the north of the city there is one such establishment that is patronised by numerous uranian Israelite women who drink coffee, chat, read newspapers, play cards and, especially, chess, every day between four and six in the afternoon.

In summer there are always particular outdoor drinking spots in which uranians gather in large numbers while avoiding others, at least in groups. In some of these concert gardens, both female and male prostitution can be observed.

In one of the most elegant Berlin concert halls a few summers back the antics of the homosexuals had grown so grave that criminal officers were summoned to bring an end to that thoughtless behaviour for which no reprimand is too harsh.

To its credit, the Berlin police force has very few *agents provocateurs* among its ranks. Certainly it would be easy for officers to find homosexuals by projecting themselves likewise, and apparently in earlier times this did indeed happen. I know of only one such incident and it took place in precisely that concert hall; a uranian saw a criminal officer observing him and, believing him to be one of his own kind making advances towards him, suffered no small shock when the officer responded to his tender caress by arresting him, bringing him to the police station and later charging him with 'assault'. As well as these venues there are a significant number patronised exclusively by uranians. It is very difficult to accurately estimate their number. Medical Officer Näcke[36] might well be right when he states that there are more than twenty uranian taverns in Berlin. Time and again in my practice I hear passing mention of uranian establishments previously unknown to me.

Each of these businesses has an additional defining characteristic; one attracts older, another younger clients, another young and old alike. Almost all of them are well patronised and on Saturday evenings and Sundays most are overflowing. Publicans, waiters, piano players, cabaret singers are themselves – almost without exception – homosexual.

You can witness homosexuals from the provinces arriving at such drinking spots for the first time, weeping in profound emotional convulsion.

Everything is thoroughly respectable in all of these taverns; here and there the criminal police or their secret agents are sent to check on things, but only very rarely has there been cause for police intervention.

Rudolf Presber[37] recently published a descriptive account of one such uranian tavern in a feuilleton article entitled 'Metropolis Types'. He wrote:

> The last stop on this interesting nocturnal journey was an elegant restaurant[38]. No shabby, sticky steps leading down, rather clean scrubbed steps leading up. A better location, a better locale. The space is decorated in a cosy manner and not without warmth. The walls are decked with paintings in gold frames. Instead of the ghastly orchestrion[39], present in almost every other tavern, there is a respectable piano with a stack of scores next to it. And playing it is a perfectly tolerable pianist accompanied by a gaunt youth with a scrappy beard, feminine of gesture with a smile

of feigned sweetness, a broad-brimmed lady's hat with a flowing veil on his pomaded head[40]. The youth sings – falsetto. The two rooms are filled with guests. Not a bad clientele, it would seem. No-one is spitting on the floor, picking his teeth with toothpicks, cleaning his ears or scratching his leg, as we have cringingly observed elsewhere this evening. A few dignified older gentlemen, a few clean-shaven sporty types, a few artists with hair hennaed and set. The naive might not notice anything awry at first. He might merely be taken aback that the second singer is also singing falsetto. He might perhaps be astonished that there is not a single female in the amply filled locale, where the customers drink moderately at neatly laid tables. Not a single indecent word is spoken, not a single song ends in a smutty punchline. There is instead a sentimental feeling cast over this thoughtfully attentive gathering. And when one of the falsetto singers, hips waggling as though he were waving full, rustling female skirts, ends a melodious little song, one of the distinguished looking old gentlemen at our table turns to one of our party, taps him with tender familiarity on the arm and humbly asks, his eyes peculiarly aglow, 'are you enjoying yourself here with us?'.

No villains here, no criminals apt to assault or rob. Unfortunate, disenfranchised, they drag the curse of nature's secret riddle through their lonely lives. People who in the daylight have sought and won respectable positions. Working honestly, their respectability never questioned, their word and name valued, they must nonetheless gather furtively and secretly under the weight of a legislative paragraph of medieval cruelty, far from their normal, happy fellow citizens, to acknowledge their insuperable drives among like-minded people, constantly threatened by the law, by contempt, by the blackmailer's malice.

With genuine sympathy in our healthy hearts for these sick individuals regarded as criminals by a remnant of medieval folly, we step out onto the quiet street. On this cloudless July night the starry sky stretches out across the moonstruck roofs. A night watchman sidles past the dark houses, his huge bunch of keys jangling. In a doorway a couple fervently hold hands. The sound of the falsetto grows distant, ever distant...

So reports Presber. Another uranian tavern that we enter is formed of four sizeable rooms. There are few free places. In the second and fourth rooms are pianos, in one 'the angels' present the latest songs, in the other there is dancing; not man and woman, but man and man. They dance with evident devotion, the female of the pair pressing languidly against the male partner; the music, though poor, truly materialises within them; they are drunk on melody, in aural bliss, but when the pianist stops they seem to wake to raw reality.

The coffee circles that often take place in these establishments are particularly distinctive. The publican, the cabaret singer or a regular may be celebrating a birthday, inviting his 'girlfriends' to celebrate the occasion. The guests appear at the agreed afternoon hour, mostly uranians from the ranks of tradesmen and labourers. Each gives the birthday boy a gift, a home-made offering, a sample of their culinary skills, a few flowers either artificial or natural. The greetings are particularly spirited, a tender curtsey or bow followed by a decorous, friendly kiss on the cheek. How they then twirl and fuss, exchange compliments, pull out their hatpins, hitch up their skirts, straighten out their waistbands, make as if to lay out their non-existent trains, and then finally utter the words, 'have you heard, my dear,' thus launching a gaiety that defies description. Particular delight and reverence are reserved for the 'dignitaries', such as the 'Baroness', the 'Directress', 'Madame Chambre Séparée'[41], while latecomers are greeted with ribald abuse. An hour later, once one is 'summoned', the entire party take their places at the tables where they devour mountains of cake and streams of coffee at an astonishing speed, the chattering and twittering, laughing, whooping and shrieking rising to a height of confusion that would strike fear into the heart of any manly guest. Having exhausted the organs of mastication and speech they bring out the handwork that they have brought along, and they crochet, knit, embroider and sew, the entertainment consisting solely of songs, recitations and recitals, all bearing witness to the artistic gifts seldom lacking in uranian gatherings.

But the climax of the evening comes when the birthday boy is graciously led to the grand piano to loud applause from all present and in a melodious alto sings his love song 'Oh, If Only I Were a Thief'[42] with as much longing as improbability. Not a false note mars the innocent revels of these few fleeting hours, until dinner time sends the lively crowd scattering in all directions.

Anyone hearing the conversation in these taverns for the first time will be surprised by the number of female names to be heard, many of them quite singular. One soon becomes aware that these are nicknames the guests use for each other. The reasons for this widespread custom vary; for one thing, most of those gathered here choose to keep their real names secret for readily comprehensible reasons, so that if others refer to them they must use these self-fashioned designations. Moreover, one instinctively feels that the sobriquet 'Herr So-and-So' presents too stark a contrast to the feminine nature of many – but by no means all – of the guests, and finally the choice of nickname also offers the Berliner a welcome opportunity to satisfy his deep-seated instinct for jokes and humour. But in many of the more virile uranian circles they frown upon the use of such female names.

Often these names are a simple female refiguring of the respective male Christian name; so Paul becomes Paula, Fritz becomes Frieda, Erich becomes Erika, Georg becomes Georgette, Theodor becomes Dorchen or Thea, and Otto becomes Ottilie or Otéro[43]. In a Berlin uranian song, in which a mother discovers that her son is 'perverse' and hurries to comfort him, he bears witness to his normality by showing her the love letters addressed to him by 'Luise', ending with the lines:

At the doorway I kissed her farewell,
But what I thought I never could tell,
For dear Mama, she would never twig,
That my Luise was really Ludwig.

These female names are often appended with differentiating additions; so for example there is a Twangy Juste[44], a Lardy Juste, a Hairpin Juste, a Frock Juste, Glove Juste and Flower Juste, a Lanky Anna, a Ballroom Anna and a Blue Plush Anna, a Doggy Lotte and a Squeaky Lotte, a Lacy Karoline and a Crash Karoline (his lively arm gestures ensure he smashes at least one glass of beer a night), a Butter Riecke, a Cheesy Klara, a Lousy Paula, a Harper Jule and a Death's Head Marie.

Many uranians receive old German epithets, such as Hildegarde, Kunigunde, Thusnelda, Schwanhilde or Adelheid, or illustrious aristocratic names like Wally von Trauten, Berta von Brunneck, Asta von Schönermark or even more magnificent names; in their taverns you find the Margravine, the Landgravine, the Burggravine and the Princess (because they live in the Markgrafen-, Landgrafen-, Burggrafen- or Kurfürstenstrasse), the Marquise de la place d'Alexandre (who lives on Alexanderplatz), the Duchess of Aschaffenburg, the Duchess d'Angoulême, the Grand-Duchess Olga, Queen Natalie, Carmen Sylva[45], the Coffee Queen, the Polish Queen, the Mistress of the Stables, Her Excellency and the empresses Messalina and Catherine.

Some names are derived from the bearer's profession; one uranian ballet dancer answers to 'Jettchen

Toe-lift', a ladies' dressmaker is 'Jenny Whalebone' and a female impersonator 'Pocahontas, the Eastern Nightingale'.

I should note that all of the nicknames mentioned here were collected by two informants in a short space of time in one single uranian locale in Berlin. Among the epithets drawn from zoology they found the 'Swiss Cow', the 'Guinea Pig', the 'Plaster Cat' (applied to one who powders heavily), the 'Teal', the 'Duck Waddle' (because he 'waddles' when he walks), the 'Black Hen', the 'Hooded Crow', the 'Shrew', 'Spectacled Cobra' and the 'Cross Spider'. And from the world of botany come the 'Blue Violet', the 'Little Reseda Bud', 'Paprika' (also known as 'Pap Reeker'), the 'Raisin', and the 'Grieving Grape' (because he is so easily moved to tears).

There is a great tendency to add a feminine or diminutive ending to titles or prominent characteristics in a highly original manner; the manager becomes the 'Manageress', the privy councillor the 'Councileress', a lawyer is a 'Lawyerette', a distinguished uranian who frequently dines in a private dining room with his friends is called 'Chambrette Separée', another, a devotee of sunbathing, is 'Tan-gerine', while a pianist is 'Pianette', another given to make up is 'Vermilionette' and an electrical engineer simply 'Electricia'.

One unusual group calls itself the 'Soldier Queens', their nicknames frequently derived from the particular regiment to which they have the greatest attachment. There's an 'Uhlan Juste', a 'Dragoon Bride', a 'Cuirassier Anna', a 'Gunnerette', even a 'Shooting Schoolgirl', whose name stems from a habit of frequenting locales near shooting schools.

Other Berlin nicknames are less readily categorised, including 'Minnehaha, the Smiling Waters', 'Rebekka, Mother of the Regiment', 'Anita with the Fangs', 'Cleo de Merde'[46], 'Little Trudy Dogbirth', 'Saint Beryllis', 'Brother in Harms', the 'Free Swiss', the 'Good Match', the 'Exalted Lady', the 'Rollmop Queen', 'Soapsuds Susanne, the 'White Wall' (a heavy user of powder), 'Rotunda'[47], 'Latrine Blossom' (the names of two uranians said to frequent public lavatories more often than necessity requires), the 'Woodsman', the 'Mother Wolf', 'Violetta', 'Aurora', 'Melitta', 'Rosaura', 'Kassandra', 'Goulash', the 'Foremother', the 'Tomb Bride', the 'Evening Star' and the 'Morning Star' because he, as the saying goes 'has gold in his mouth', that is, teeth fitted with gold fillings[48].

Female uranians use similar names among themselves, particularly in their locales, of which there is also no small number. In contrast to the men, however, they usually use simple first names, rarely a nickname referencing a particular characteristic of the bearer. One-syllable names are preferred, such as Fritz, Heinz, Max, Franz and especially Hans; however others answer to Arthur, Edmund, Theo, Oskar, Roderich or Rudolf.

A remarkable number of female uranians take their names from history and literature, of the Berliners suffice it to mention Napoleon, Nero, Caesar, Heliogabalus, Caligula, Antinous, Gregory, Carlos, Posa, Mortimer, Götz, Tasso, Egmont, Armin, Teja, Blücher, Ofterdingen, Karl Moor, Franz Lerse, Jörn Uhl, Don Juan, Puck and Hiddigeigei.

Less distinguished nicknames for female uranians include Bubi, Rollmop, Caraway Fritz and Bacon Emil.

Among Berlin's uranian drinking spots, its 'soldier taverns' merit particular attention. Usually located near barracks, they are busiest in the hours between going-home time and taps. Around then you can see up to 50 soldiers in these establishments, including non-commissioned officers, who have come to seek out a homosexual to pick up their tab, and rarely do they return to barracks without getting what they came for. These establishments seldom last. Before long an unidentified person blows the whistle, usually motivated by envy or revenge, and they are almost always forbidden on orders of the regiment. One or two will arise soon after, and sometimes there are several similar establishments in the same area. Only recently a typical soldier pub in the south-west of the city named the 'Katzenmutter'[49] was rumbled; I do not know if the unusual name came from the old landlady, whose slinking gait and round, whiskery face betrayed something of the feline, or from the cats that jumped around the tables and chairs and whose likenesses graced the walls of the unusual establishment.

Were a normally sexed person to enter such an establishment, he might be puzzled to see so many finely dressed men sitting there with soldiers, though he would find nothing particularly offensive. The friendships between homosexuals and soldiers forged here over sausage, salad and beer frequently endure for the full term of service, and often longer. The soldier returns home, living as a married farmer far from his beloved

Berlin garrison, but many a uranian still receives freshly killed quarry as a token of friendship. Sometimes these relationships are even passed on to younger brothers; I know one case where a homosexual had relations with three brothers one after the other, all of whom were with the Cuirassiers.

His day's service at an end, the soldier usually goes home to his friend, who has already prepared his favourite meal for him with his own two hands, which the soldier hungrily wolfs down in great quantities. Then the young warrior, in the pink of health, takes up a goodly part of the sofa, while the uranian, humbly perched on a chair, darns the torn clothes he has brought with him or knits the Christmas stockings with which he indents to surprise his beloved, although keeping them secret presents a considerable challenge to the happy lover's self-restraint.

All the while they discuss the little details of royal service; what the 'old man' (the captain) said at muster, what the next day will bring, what the coming sentry duty holds and whether he might be seen marching past in the coming days. Finally the lover accompanies the soldier to a spot near the barracks, but not before filling his flask with wine and packing his sandwiches.

On parade mornings, the uranian stands on Belle-Alliance-Strasse[50] at the agreed spot bright and early to secure a place in the front row. Hopefully his soldier is a flank man so he can get a good look at him. And afterwards he holds out until he comes home again, and in the evening he has leave, then they go to the 'Busch' Circus[51], after the soldier drops his 50 pfennig day bonus in his friend's money box.

An even greater event is the 'Kaiser's Birthday Company Pleasure'. That is when the homosexual accompanies his friend as a 'cousin'. With touching bliss he dances with the girl who has just danced with his soldier; he has no idea what she looks like because he only had eyes for his soldier and thinks only of him as he holds her. Probably the captain too will speak to him as the cousin of a private or non-commissioned officer. But it can also come to pass that the homosexual must stay away from the celebration, to his dismay, because a few days previously he attended the same banquet as one of the officers present.

It is not difficult to see why soldiers might entertain relations with homosexuals. For one, it is a desire to make life in the metropolis more comfortable for themselves, to have better food, more drinks, cigars and pleasures (dancehalls, theatre, and such). Moreover, the soldier – often a farmer, tradesman or labourer of minimal education – profits mentally from relations with the homosexual, who gives him good books, talks to him about current events, takes him to museums, points out what is appropriate and what is not, while the merry, witty nature that many uranians share contributes to his amusement. In his naivety he is heartily entertained when his friend sings him couplets or even dances for him with a lampshade as a bonnet and an apron arranged to maidenly effect. Other reasons might be lack of money, or of maidens – at least those who do not charge – the fear of venereal diseases which are so frowned upon by the military, and his earnest intention to remain true to his bride at home, to whom he swore fidelity in parting and whose every anxious letter reminds him of this oath.

Near such taverns there is also often a 'military beat', where soldiers go alone or in pairs to make contact with homosexuals. Here I wish to point out a significant phenomenon, of which a well-travelled homosexual made me aware, and whose accuracy has been unanimously confirmed to me on enquiry by reliable informants since then – that is, that 'soldier prostitutes' are more prevalent in countries where there is greater legal persecution of homosexuals. Clearly this is related to the fact that in countries where the statute books affect uranians, soldiers have less to fear from blackmail and other nuisances.

Apart from London, where numerous soldiers prostitute themselves in unambiguous fashion in the most popular parks and streets from late afternoon until after midnight, our informant claims never to have found such a selection of soldiers of various branches, every evening, as in Berlin. There are around half a dozen places where soldiers parade back and forth with intent after the fall of dusk. Just like locales, the 'beats' also change fairly often; soldiers were recently barred from one such popular thoroughfare, the Planufer[52].

Soldier prostitution is particularly prevalent in the Scandinavian capitals; in recent years Stockholm military patrols have investigated soldiers 'loitering' for said purpose, but this, as our informant who has lived for some time in the Swedish capital assures us, has done little to ease the situation.

The Finnish capital of Helsinki, with around 80,000 inhabitants, offers especially pronounced military prostitution. It is also seen to a lesser extent in Saint Petersburg, where sailors, particularly, make the acquaintance of homosexuals in a square far from the city centre.

Our informant draws a comparison with the city of Paris, reporting that 'in 18 months only the suggestion of a military beat' was to be found and, discovering a similar state of affairs in Amsterdam, Brussels, Rome, Milan, Naples and Florence (all cities without uranian laws), concludes 'that in every European country with strict penal provisions against homosexual activities, the way soldiers offer themselves is something difficult to believe until you have seen it with your own eyes, whereas in countries without uranian laws you find almost nothing of the sort'.

However the customary designation of 'soldier prostitution' does not conform to the usual definition of prostitution because for the soldiers it is certainly not a 'professional or commercial application of the body'. Here I should like to correct the widespread opinion that relations between soldiers and homosexuals are ordinarily predicated on acts that are punishable in and of themselves. If it should come to the sexual act, and that is not at all so in every case, this usually takes the form of arousal through embrace, pressing against one another and touching of body parts, as is ordinarily the case in homosexual activities. The idea that homosexuals, particularly the more feminine ones, are pederasts[53] in the common sense, is completely erroneous. An episode transpired in my practice recently which illustrated to me how prevalent this opinion is, even in Berlin. In the wake of my statistical survey[54] on the extent of uranianism there was much discussion of homosexuality in the newspapers, and a conservative master butcher from the east came to visit me, an utterly normal family man, who in all earnestness introduced himself with the following words: 'For some weeks now I have had a strong itch near my anus and I should like you to examine it to see if I have homosexual inclinations'.

The rarity of truly pederastic acts does nothing to diminish the cruelty and injustice of the relevant penal provisions, because it is the preliminary investigation that is so catastrophic, and the court – when it hands down a sentence, even if it is right to do so – does not restrict itself as narrowly as it should to the particular nature of the activity. And so I repeat here that the purely sexual moment in the life and love of the homosexual plays no greater part than it does in non-uranian life; the intimate and private nature of this issue is such that I would never address it in my observations were it not for the advocates of false morality who keep drawing it to the forefront as the principal issue.

There is another grouping in Berlin that has long enjoyed diverse relations with uranians – athletes. The numerous athletes' associations in the capital are largely comprised of unmarried working class men between 18 and 25; their ranks are dominated by locksmiths, blacksmiths and various other metal workers. Strength, danger and audacity are everything to such people. In their eyes 'the fight between Russia and Japan[55] is nothing of the sort because there is too much shooting and not enough wrestling, stabbing and boxing'.

We now enter an athletic club which has a homosexual dimension. In the back room of a small inn men are 'drilling'. The small room is scented with the curious amalgam of oil, metal and sweat that iron workers often exude. There are iron bars, dumbbells, weights of 100 pounds and more on the floor alongside mattresses where the wrestlers wrangle. There are eight to ten strapping athletes here, some in black jerseys, some baring their bodies, their chests and arms tattooed.

On the window side of the room is a long, narrow table surrounded by benches where a number of men sit, their distinguished features and their suits presenting a strange contrast to the strongmen. At the head of the table sits the Madam President or Protectress of the athletic club, a dressmaker who calls to mind Martial's saying 'that with one small exception he inherited everything from his mother'. The neophyte would never imagine him to be a member of the athletic club – let alone its Madam President.

On the table is a money box into which each guest makes a modest contribution to the expenses, and the purchase of weights and mattresses. They also cover the tab for the athletes – the seltzer water, lemonade and cigarettes before and during exercises, and the beer and supper after weightlifting and wrestling.

The uranian friends ensure that the exercises are practised diligently, the expert patrons avidly observing the sculptural beauty of the movements and the play of muscles, spiritedly critiquing each 'passage'.

One particular reason that some homosexuals form bonds with athletes is that should they be harassed in any way, or blackmailed as a result of the invidious Paragraph 175, they need sturdy, fearless men on their side on whose protection and 'active' friendship they might rely.

Landlords of establishments both uranian and otherwise stage major uranian balls in the wintertime, which in their nature and extent are a true speciality of Berlin. High officials treat them as an interesting attraction[56], bringing distinguished aliens – foreigners, in other words – who wish to see something extraordinary in the youngest of the European metropolises. They have already been the subject of numerous studies, such as the recent report by Oscar Méténier in *Vertus et Vices allemands, les Berlinois chez eux*[57]. In the high season between October and Easter there are numerous such balls in any given week, sometimes more than one in a single evening. Although the entrance fee is rarely less than one and a half marks, these events are usually well attended. Undercover police officers are almost always on hand to prevent unseemly activity; as far as I am aware, however, there has never been cause for intervention. The organisers are under instruction to, as far as possible, only admit those known to them as homosexual.

Some of the balls have a particular reputation, particularly the one staged after New Year's, at which new and often home-made outfits are presented. With a few fellow doctors, I attended one of these balls last year where there were some 800 guests. At around 10 in the evening the major venues are still empty. Only after 11 do they begin to fill. Many visitors are in visiting or street clothes, but many more are costumed. Some of them arrive well concealed by impenetrable domino masks, they come and go without anyone suspecting their identity. Others remove their masks at midnight, some come in fantastical robes, many in ladies' clothing, some simply attired, others in sumptuous costumes. I saw one South American in a Parisian robe said to have cost over 2000 francs.

More than a few seem so feminine in their appearance and movements that even cognoscenti have difficulty recognising them as men. I recall one such ball which I attended with a criminal constable who was very experienced in these areas, where we observed a servant whom this officer was utterly convinced was a real woman, and I too had only the slightest doubt, until I spoke to her and it became apparent that she was a 'man'. There are few real women at these balls, and only when a uranian brings his landlady, a female friend or – his wife. Male uranians are not generally as strict as they are at the corresponding female uranian balls where 'real men' are strictly barred from entry. The most distasteful, repellent sight at these balls are the considerable number of homosexuals who, although boasting stately moustaches or even full beards, come as 'women'. The finest costumes are greeted with thunderous fanfare on the signal of the moderator, who leads their bearers through the hall. The flow of guests usually reaches its zenith between midnight and one o'clock. Around two o'clock comes a coffee break – the main source of income for the proprietors. In the space of a few minutes long tables are set up and decked, and several hundred guests take their places; a few humorous songs and dances season the entertainment, and then the gleeful whirl starts up again, continuing until morning.

In one of the large halls in which the uranians stage their balls, barely a week passes without a similar evening ball for female uranians, many of whom dress in men's clothing. The largest gathering of homosexual women is an annual costume party arranged by a lady of Berlin. This party is not open to the public, rather it is usually restricted to those acquainted with the ladies of the committee. One participant, Miss R., sketched the following depiction for me:

After eight on a fine winter's evening, coach after coach pulls up in front of one of Berlin's finest hotels, from which emerge women and men in costumes of every land and epoch. Here you see a stylish fraternity member arriving with impressive duelling scars[58], there a slim Rococo cavalier gallantly helping a lady alight from her coach. The large, brightly lit rooms become ever more crowded; here comes a fat Capuchin monk, accepting the salutations of respectful gypsies, pierrots, sailors, clowns, bakers, peasants, spruce officers, gentlemen and ladies in riding outfits, Boers, Japanese gentlemen and dainty geishas. A dark-eyed Carmen sets a jockey aflame, a fiery Italian strikes up an intimate friendship with a snowman. The cheerful gaggle of those in the most colourful, dazzling costumes presents an unusually becoming tableau. The partygoers first fortify themselves at the flower-laden tables. The host, in a smart velvet jacket,

welcomes the gathering in a brief, pithy address.
Then the tables are cleared away. The 'Waves
of the Danube' waltz starts up, and the couples
swing through the night in circles accompanied
by cheerful dance tunes. From the adjoining halls
comes the sound of bright laughter, the clinking of
glasses and blithe song, but nowhere – no matter
where you look – are the bounds of an elegant
costume party transgressed. Not a single false note
brings disharmony to the general merriment, until
the last of the guests steps out into the wan dawn
light of a cold February morning from a venue
where, for just a few hours, they were able to find
sympathetic company with which to live the dream
of their innermost feelings. Anyone who had the
opportunity of attending such a party would spend
the rest of his life in honest conviction defending
uranian women so wrongly condemned, because it
would be apparent that good and bad people are to
be found everywhere, that the natural homosexual
inclination is no less apt to mark a person out as
either good or evil than the heterosexual.

Just as well attended as the balls, 'gentlemen's
evenings' are theatrical events that are occasionally
staged by uranians, for uranians. Usually the entire cast
of artistes are 'intermediaries'; especially popular are the
homosexual parodies of renowned literary works, and
there is no little jollity when the angels perform as Marthe
Schwertlein[59], when 'Harper Jule' plays Salome, or when
Schwanhilde plays Mary Stuart, Queen Elizabeth and

the nurse[60] all in one.

As well as restaurants, Berlin also has hotels, guesthouses and bathing facilities that are almost exclusively patronised by homosexuals; however I have yet to identify the Berlin community house for homosexuals recently mentioned by Pastor Philipps[61].

Homosexuality in bathing facilities is not nearly as widespread in Berlin as it is in other major cities, particularly Saint Petersburg[62] and Vienna. In the Austrian capital there is a bathhouse that on certain days is so overrun with homosexuals that they make up the entirety of the clientele[63]. In Berlin I know of four medium-sized bathing facilities that survive solely on their homosexual customers. There are also certain swimming pools that at particular times become meeting places for homosexuals.

In these facilities, as well as in the restaurants and hotels, the proprietors and employees are often themselves homosexual. However, they are not as a rule attracted to the work with the intention of making uranian acquaintances or even to abet fornication (as defined by Paragraph 180[64] of the Criminal Code), rather it gradually gets around that the proprietor or the head waiter or a masseur is 'one of them', which then draws uranians in greater number, because they feel more at ease there.

The proprietors are often not entirely aware that they could fall afoul of the 'procuration' paragraphs of the Criminal Code. Recently a trial concerning homosexual procuration attracted a good deal of attention; it was brought against an old uranian who ran a pension in the west of the city which was predominantly patronised by homosexual ladies and gentlemen. Although the defendants – not without cause, in my opinion – pointed out that they neither charged nor received higher prices than is usual for comparable establishments, nor felt themselves authorised to monitor what their guests (who included a well-known member of the Reichstag) did in their rooms with others, they were both sentenced to one month's prison.

A much greater risk is run by proprietors of hotels where male prostitutes arrive with their gentlemen for a few hours, or the uranian flophouses, of which Berlin evidently has a considerable number. These locales are a direct consequence of the conditions created by Paragraph 175. They are particularly favoured by uranians from the higher social circles, as well as uranian officers of foreign garrisons, who turn to trustworthy persons who can offer them something 'completely safe', out of a well-founded fear of falling into the hands of blackmailers, criminals or traitors.

In Brussels this last summer a shoemaker and his wife were arrested after they were found with numerous albums of photographs that they would present for selection on enquiry. Similar things have been known in Berlin. A credible source relayed to me that there are intermediaries with whom men – verbally, in writing, even by telegraph – place orders for people, specifying every imaginable fetishistic hobby, cuirassiers with white trousers and high boots, men in women's clothing, women in men's clothing, brewer's draymen, stone-carriers in work clothes, even chimney sweeps. Their requests are almost always fulfilled at the determined time. Similar agencies exist for uranian ladies.

Although they may be unaware of it, Berlin's daily newspapers also frequently act as go-betweens. In many papers, nearly every day you can find several classified advertisements that serve homosexual ends, such as 'young lady seeks female friend', 'young man seeks male friend'. These are a few examples of such announcements taken from Berlin newspapers of all political stripes in recent times[65].

> Older gentleman, no ladies' man, seeks
> acquaintance with kindred spirits. Repl. to S.O.
> 2099

> Older bachelor looking for like-minded
> 'connection', Morgenpost Bülowstrasse

> Gentleman, 23, seeks friend. Write to 'Sokrates'
> at forwarding centre Kochstrasse.

> Bachelor, good co., seeks friendly exchange with
> single, like-minded older gentleman. Off. A. B.
> 11 P.O. 76.

> Young educ. man, 29 years old, seeks friendly
> exchange with energetic, masterful, well-situated
> gentleman. Letters requested at TWL mailing
> department for this paper.

> Young lady, respectable, 24 years old, seeks pretty

young lady as friend. Offers requested at no.
3654 to the mailing department.

Lady, 36, seeks friendly exchange. PO 16, 'Plato'.

Bosom friend, pleasant, seeks spirited, vivacious
lady, 23. Psyche, PO 69.

Seeking educ. friend, early 30s, preferably blond.
Offers to H. R. 1622 at this paper

Seamstress, 22, seeks 'friend', PO 33.

Such notices, I have been assured by numerous
sources, are very well understood by their intended
readers.

The issue of male prostitution has already come
up on several occasions, and we really cannot avoid this
lamentable practice if we wish to produce a more or less
comprehensive account of the diverse forms in which
uranian life manifests itself in Berlin.

Like any other metropolis, Berlin has both
female and male prostitution. The two are closely related
in their origins, nature, causes and consequences. Here,
as elsewhere, there are two reasons that always come
together, of which one or the other soon prevails: inner
inclination and outward circumstances. Those who fall
prey to prostitution are marked from youth onwards by
certain peculiarities of which the most pronounced is an
urge for fine living combined with a tendency to laziness.
If the external circumstances are favourable to these

qualities, that is, if the parents are well-off, the young person will be safe from prostitution. But if there is domestic squalor, a miserable livelihood, unemployment, lack of accommodation and possibly the greatest of all problems, hunger, then stable, steadfast characters might well withstand, but the weaker will seek out the ever-present temptation, succumb to it and sell themselves, ignoring their mothers' tears.

There are humanitarians who expect improvement to come from freedom of the will and others from force of circumstances; one longs for education and religion, the other looks to the state of the future. Both are overly optimistic. Those who wish to help must strive to improve conditions from within and without, such that girls and youths are not obliged to sell themselves, and help improve people with particular consideration for the laws of inheritance, so that the obligation to sell oneself as a product falls away.

You might say that is impossible, but I say he who surrenders is lost.

Prostitution's sphere of activity is the street, particular areas and squares, the so-called 'beats'. A homosexual showed me a map of Berlin on which he had marked the 'beats' in blue; the number of places thus designated was not inconsiderable.

Since time immemorial the various parts of the Tiergarten[66] have played their own particular part. There is no other forest that is so interwoven with human destiny as this park measuring over 1000 acres.

It is not the beauty of its landscape nor its artistic ornaments that lend it significance, but people

– their lives, loves and laments. From early morning, when the well-to-do work off their meals on horseback, until midday, when the Kaiser undertakes his ride[67]; from early afternoon, when thousands of children play in the park, until late afternoon, when the bourgeoisie goes strolling, each pathway has its own character, in every season, in every hour. If Emile Zola had lived in Berlin I do not doubt that he would have investigated these woods and that his enquiries would have resulted in another *Germinal*.

But when evening falls and the sun turns to other worlds, the breath of dusk mingles with the questing, yearning breath from millions of earthly beings, all part of that global spirit that some call the spirit of fornication but which in truth is just a fragment of the great, powerful drive, higher than everything, lower than anything, which ceaselessly shapes, prevails, forges and forms.

Couples meet at every crossroads in the Tiergarten – see how they hasten to one another, how joyfully they greet each other and stride into the future pressed close in conversation, see how they alight at the now empty benches and silently embrace, and how the high, inalienable kind of love sits side-by-side with the more vendible variety.

Women offer themselves for sale on three widely distributed paths, the men on two. While female and male prostitution are intertwined, here each has its own 'beat'. Of the men's, one is filled every evening almost exclusively by cavalrymen, their sabres glinting queerly in the dark, while the other, quite a long stretch, is largely occupied by those reckless lads apt to refer to themselves in Berlin dialect as 'nice and naughty'. Here you will find one of the typical half-moon-shaped Tiergarten benches, where from midnight onwards thirty prostitutes and homeless lads sit close to each other, some fast asleep, others yelling and shrieking. They call this bench the 'art exhibition'. Now and then a man comes along, strikes a match and illuminates the row.

Not infrequently the lads' shrieking is interrupted by a shrill cry, a call for help from one robbed or manhandled in the thicket, or the snatches of music wafting over from the Zelten[68] are punctuated by a sharp bang, reporting of one who has answered the question of life in the negative.

And anyone looking for the colourful city characters erroneously reported to be extinct will find no shortage of them in the Tiergarten. See the old lady there by the waters of Neuer See with the four dogs? For forty years, with brief intermissions during the summer, she has been taking the same walk at the same time, always alone, ever since her husband died of a haemorrhage on her wedding day in transit from the registry office to the church. That desiccated, hunched apparition with the shaggy grey beard? He is a Russian baron who seeks out a solitary bench, sits down and cries 'rab, rab, rab', a sound much like the crowing of a raven. This mating call draws the odd 'cheeky grafter' from obscure paths – his friends, to whom he distributes the 'dough' left over from his daily earnings, usually three to five marks.

Male prostitutes can be divided into two groups – those who are normally sexed and those who are themselves homosexual, or 'genuine'. The latter are often particularly feminine, and some occasionally wear women's clothes, a practice met with particular disfavour by female prostitutes. This is ordinarily the only *casus belli* between the two groups, because experience has shown that neither would rob the other of clientele were it not for this fraudulent representation. I once asked a fairly well educated prostitute to explain the good relations between female and male prostitutes. 'We know that every john wants what he wants,' she answered.

There are often unusual pairings among Berlin prostitutes. Normal male prostitutes, the so-called doll-boys, not infrequently conduct cooperative 'work' with normal female prostitutes. I have even heard tell of pairs of siblings of whom both sister and brother fall prey to this lowly work; often two female and not infrequently two male prostitutes will cohabit, and finally there are also cases of female homosexual prostitutes who take male homosexual prostitutes as pimps, finding them to be less brutal than their heterosexual colleagues.

It is established fact that there is a large number of homosexuals among female prostitutes, estimated at 20 per cent. Some might wonder at this apparent contradiction, after all commercial prostitution primarily serves the sexual satisfaction of the male. Often it is said that they suffer from surfeit, but that is not actually the case, because it has been proven that these girls usually know themselves to be homosexual before taking up prostitution, and the fact of their homosexuality only serves to prove that selling their bodies is simply seen as a business, one they regard with cool calculation.

The relationships between prostitutes are noteworthy. Even here the system of double morality has made its presence felt. Because while the manly, active partner, the 'father', is at liberty, free to pursue female contact beyond the shared bedchamber, he demands the utmost fidelity from the 'female', passive partner when it comes to homosexual activity. When this fidelity is breached he exposes himself to the most grievous abuse. It also comes to pass that the manly partner forbids the womanly partner from pursuing work for the duration of their affair.

The female street prostitutes of Berlin also maintain diverse relations with uranian women of the better social circles, and on the street they might even make advances to women who seem homosexual. Here it is worth noting that the fees for women are much lower, and might indeed be waived altogether in some instances. One young lady who certainly appears decidedly homosexual reported to me that prostitutes had made her offers of 20 marks and more on the street.

The poor example of both female and male prostitution is not just a threat to public morality, and to public health – for it is far from uncommon that infectious diseases from scabies to syphilis are passed through male prostitution – but also public safety to a large degree.

Prostitution and criminality go hand in hand; theft and burglary, blackmail and coercion, forgery and embezzlement, every sort of violence; in short, every possible crime against person or property are a way of life for most male prostitutes, and what is particularly hazardous is that in most cases the anxious homosexual fails to report such crimes.

While twenty of Berlin's uranian population of 50,000 souls – this figure is surely not too high – are caught on average by the 'long arm of the law' every year, at least a hundred times more, that is, 2000 a year, fall victim to blackmailers who, as the Berlin Criminal Police will gladly attest, have built a widespread and particularly profitable profession from the exploitation of the homosexual nature.

The close links between prostitutes and criminals also arise from their use of the same shared criminal jargon. If the 'beat boys' are looking for their quarry, they call it 'going on a collection tour', blackmail itself they designate in various degrees: 'scalding', 'burning', 'busting', 'fleecing', 'clipping', 'dusting down', 'plucking' and 'clamping'. Here it is worth noting that in Berlin there are also criminals who specialise in 'plucking' male prostitutes by threatening them with a charge of pederasty or blackmail. They categorise the 'schwul [69] groups' according to liquidity into 'mutts'[70], 'stumps' and 'gentlemen', and the looted money they refer to as 'ashes', 'wire', 'dimes', 'gravel', 'rags', 'dosh', 'meschinne', 'monnaie', 'moss', 'quid', 'plates', 'powder', 'loot', 'dough', 'cinnamon', and for gold coins, 'silent monarchs'. To have money means 'to be in shape', to have none is 'to be dead', should something get in their way they say that 'the tour has been messed up', 'bunking' means running away, 'snuffing it' is dying, and if they are picked up by the 'claws' – the criminal police, 'the blues', or policemen – they call it 'going up', 'flying up', 'running out', 'crashing' or 'going flat'. That is when they are brought to the 'cops', or the police station, then to the 'nick', the remand prison, and finally, as the euphemism goes, they move to the 'Berlin suburbs', understood as Tegel, Plötzensee and Rummelsburg[71], the locations of prisons and work houses. Only rarely do they leave better than they arrived. Well-to-do uranians often try their hardest to save prostitutes from the street, but only in very few cases do they succeed. Many 'feast on memories' when they get older by 'drilling' small sums of money out of known homosexuals with whom they once crossed paths, which they refer to as 'collecting interest' or 'tapping'.

This dangerous class of individuals usually has a good sense for those who are homosexually inclined, but they also not infrequently threaten and accuse entirely normally sexed people. I offer one case as an example, which I received in writing a short while ago:

> Last autumn I was travelling through Berlin, arriving on a southbound night train and I spent a night in an area near the main station so that I might resume my travels the next morning. Taking advantage of the mild evening, I went out for a stroll.
>
> As I left the passage I noticed a group of young lads standing together, of whom one, around 20 years old, was whimpering, with a hanky pressed to his cheek. This caused me to involuntarily fix my eye on him longer than is customary, and in my sympathy I turned around to him once more, before walking up the central avenue of Unter den Linden

to make my way to the Brandenburg Gate with the aim of briefly taking in the Bismarck Memorial[72] which I had not seen before. A short while later I noticed this same man, now alone, cloth still held to his cheek, walking ahead of me before coming to a stop at a Litfaß[73] column near the Gate. I thought nothing of it and continued on my way. Then he approached me and asked for a hand-out, and in a disguised whimper implored me not to turn him over to the police, and told me a long-winded story. He came from the east, near Bromberg, he said, and had not managed to find work, was now completely penniless and had pawned his few personal effects for 16 marks; as soon as he managed to raise this sum and redeem his goods he planned to go back home. We had now come to a public convenience; to the right of the entrance I gave him 50 pfennigs with the admonition that he should work to raise the money to redeem his effects, telling him I was a stranger here myself and only passing through and that he should now continue on his way. I then entered the convenience and heard someone entering behind me, but paid no further attention. When I made to leave on the other side, however, intending to continue on my way to the Bismarck Memorial, I saw my lad grinning, this time without the cloth, blocking my way with the words 'if you don't give me 16 marks I will report you and they'll throw you in the can'. He then said, to my boundless astonishment, 'I'll report you, you rotter, for the dirty things you done to me. Give me 16

marks or I'll shout so loud the whole of bleedin'
Berlin will come running.'[74] Here I should note that
I am 58 years old, a grandfather several times over,
and am a member of the upper civil servant class.
If not my reputation, then certainly my onward
journey was in jeopardy should I became entangled
in such an investigation, especially one so sordid.

Therefore I quickly attained the edge of the
Charlottenburger Chaussee[75] and waved down an
empty cab, the lad's scurrilous patter pursuing me all
the while. Before the cab stopped, the blackmailer
shouted – his voice now completely changed, 'you
old cur, you just wait, you'll get yours'. At the same
time he made as if to mount the cab with me. A
few passers-by stopped in their tracks, but there
was not a policeman in sight. Then I reached into
my pocket, held out a ten-mark note and threw it
on the pavement in such a way that he had to walk
some distance to retrieve it. I used this moment
to jump into the cab and spurred the cabby on by
naming the main station as my destination. When
the cabby enquired about the incident I said the
man was clearly drunk and had demanded money
from me, whereupon he jovially replied, 'Yeah,
yeah, it's a den of bleedin' thieves around here. You
shouldn't've given that scavenger a pfennig.' Little
did he suspect that it was in fact ten marks. I now
decided against visiting the Bismarck Memorial,
and Berlin's other sights, but took care not to cast a
sympathetic eye on youths, with or without hankies
on their cheeks. I have no doubt at all that this

ostentatious use of the hanky is a blackmailer's trick, used to attract the attention of the passer-by and identify those susceptible to blackmail – a kind-hearted provincial such as myself, for instance.

Surely it is high time that we put an end to such criminal behaviour by repealing Paragraph 175.

Here I pick out a second typical case, which the *Norddeutsche Allgemeine Zeitung* reported on 11 November 1904:

The 10th Criminal Chamber of the Regional Court yesterday heard a case in which a degenerate individual used Paragraph 175 of the Criminal Code to attempt blackmail. The maliciously accused worker Karl R. had been bombarded with letters, over and over, from a man he had never met, letters which made all sorts of invented claims with reference to Paragraph 175 and which contained an unmistakable demand for money. The recipient at first paid no attention to these blackmail letters, wanting no contact whatsoever with such a sordid matter. But when the letters caused grave concern among his family, he brought a charge. The court sentenced the accused to three years' prison.

Finally, a third case from among so many, which is significant in more than one regard. A homosexual had followed a prostitute to his apartment; when he arrived, the latter said with steely resolve, 'I am Shirt-Sleeves Emil, a well-known blackmailer, give me your wallet'. Once he had it, he took off his coat, rolled up his sleeves to reveal obscene tattoos on his forearms, dragged the homosexual by his collar to the window of the fourth-floor apartment and threatened to cast him out if he did not hand over all the valuables he had about him. When he had convinced him that he had nothing more, the blackmailer asked how much money he needed for the return journey, 'gifted' him 50 pfennigs and 'now' – he continued – 'come with me and sink some Knallblech (champagne) – it's on me.' And he did not let him go until the homosexual had 'burnt through' a large part of that which he had 'inherited'.

How can it be that such a dangerous issue is so rarely reported? Homosexuals and most normally sexed people shy away from scandal, they know that should they bring a charge, the accused will immediately mount a counter-charge, partly for revenge, partly as justification, on the basis of Paragraph 175. Even if the well-versed Berlin criminal authorities do not yield to the statements of blackmailers and thieves, nor prostitutes in general since the understanding tenure of the late, honourable Criminal Director Meerscheidt-Hüllessem[76], to whom the uranians of the capital owe a debt of gratitude, public prosecutors and judges are often not so well informed. It happens often enough that the blackmailer is sentenced, but his victim is compromised to the utmost, disadvantaged, his status destroyed. I remember the verdict in the blackmail case of Aßmann and associates, whose victim was the unfortunate Count H., cousin of our Kaiser[77]. Indeed, I have experienced cases in which the public prosecutors have raised charges based on the statements of such individuals. One particular case has remained in my memory.

An old homosexual had brought a charge of burglary against a man whose picture he found in the Berlin Criminal Album[78]. The thief, with numerous prior convictions, lodged the counterclaim that the plaintiff had raped him in his sleep. Unbelievably, the court paid credence to his statement, swore him in as a witness, and sentenced the homosexual, who already had two prior convictions under Paragraph 175, to one year in jail. I was called as an expert witness and will never forget how the old fellow – a giant of a man – collapsed on hearing a sentence with which he had never reckoned; he raised himself up and then with a fearful shriek yelled 'judicial assassins' at the judges.

Yes, these are exceptional cases, yes, homosexuals – as a high-placed civil servant once countered and as I know from my own observations – 'already have it good' in Berlin. But there is yet more proof of the indefensibility of a law that, as a uranian recently put it to me, punishes 'the misfortune rather than the deed'. As I have already pointed out, when one considers the thoroughly discreet nature of the activities in question, and further considers that both participants, without infringing on the rights of a third party, undertake the deed solely among and with themselves, then only in entirely incidental circumstances in a vanishingly small number of exceptional cases will this become known to others.

And yet if the criminal authorities, who have several thousand names on the 'Berlin Pederast List'[79] established by Meerscheidt-Hüllessem, went after homosexuals like they went after real criminals, it would very soon result in an utter failure of implementation according to current penal provisions. This would also be the case if, as the Cologne Resolution[80] of the Evangelical Morality Association recommended, the 'truly, inherently sick' among homosexuals were delivered to sanatoria.

Here again I stress, to avoid any confusion, that these demands on behalf of homosexuals relate to nothing more than what *adults in free agreement do with each other*; and that society must of course protect against those who infringe the rights of third parties, who assault minors, against the Sternbergs and Dippolds[81] and others who use violence.

Some time ago in a Berlin teachers' newspaper[82] a teacher stated that in light of the findings of scientific research one must, for better or for worse, address the issue of how homosexuals could be incorporated into society 'in a way that accords with the goals of that society'.

But has this question not long been answered?

Where in Berlin is the culture enthusiast who has not delighted in the dramatic talents of a uranian tragedienne, a music lover who has not enjoyed the voice of a uranian lieder singer!

Think of the cook who prepares your meal, the hairdresser who attends to you, the seamstress who makes your wife's clothes and the flower seller who decorates your apartment – are you certain there is not a uranian among them?

Plunge into the masterpieces of world literature, scrutinise the heroes of history, walk in the footsteps of the great solitary thinkers, and you are certain to encounter homosexuals from time to time, one who might be dear to you and who achieved greatness despite – some even claim because of – this special quality.

Do you know for sure that among those closest to you, whom you love most tenderly, those you adore above all, whether among your best friends, your sisters and brothers – that not one is a uranian?

There is not a father or a mother who can say that not one of their children will be born to the uranian sex. I could touch on many examples here but I will restrict myself to sharing two letters, one from a father, the other from a mother.

A Berlin pedagogue, one of the 750 principals and teachers of the better teaching institutions who in 1904 joined 2,800 German doctors in signing the petition to the Reichstag demanding the repeal of the uranian paragraph, writes, 'that he until recently, having no familiarity with the subject matter at hand, would have believed in the necessity of Paragraph 175. Only after the death of a youth who rejoiced in all that was fine, true and good, who took up a revolver after he discovered his counter-sexual inclination were his eyes opened; that youth was his son.' 'A gravely afflicted father,' he concluded, 'thanks the Scientific-Humanitarian Committee[83] for its humanitarian work.'

And a mother writes:

Esteemed Sir!

In light of your intention to help those people made unfortunate by birth and further so by Paragraph 175 of the Criminal Code, allow me to direct the following questions to you, the reply to which is a matter of life and death for two people. Is there any hope that the paragraph in question will be read in the Reichstag over the course of this winter, and do you believe in the possibility that the law will be repealed? A very close relation of mine[84] is one of these unfortunates. He is a highly talented young man who with his good, righteous character, through his moral conduct has won a great deal of respect from his fellow citizens, particularly his colleagues and superiors. His great knowledge soon led him to attain a secure, well-paying position, until danger approached in the shape of the most abominable blackmailer. Unfortunately on one occasion he was weak enough to succumb to temptation. After surrendering thousands, his health suffering under the constant anxiety and fear of being discovered, he was forced to abandon everything – his homeland, his parents and his livelihood – to flee the shame. After numerous unsuccessful attempts to secure a similar position in Switzerland without a certificate of nationality, he decided to emigrate to America. There, through iron dedication and the most upright life, he planned to establish himself in a profession to which he was previously a stranger and he has already passed the necessary exams. But numerous tribulations have caused him to lose courage and he sets great store on the repeal of the paragraph in question. His father has since passed away, his only son unable to hasten to the death bed, and his mother is alone and sick at heart, with the eternal longing to see her good, unfortunate son, and is often close to despair. She would owe you a debt of limitless gratitude, noble sir, were you able to give her hope for the fulfilment of this, her greatest wish, or were you to share any other advice.

That was the mother's letter. In this and similar cases, who can help recalling the words of Goethe: 'Sacrifice is here/Not of lamb nor steer/But of human woe and human pain'[85].

Here we come to the end of our wanderings, and I thank the reader who has accompanied me for this long stretch that has brought us to so many dark chasms of human misery, but also to some great heights. Before we part, allow me to recount two more events from past and present, and then pose a question.

Once upon a time there was a prince-bishop, Philipp[86], who lived in the old city of Würzburg on the River Main. This was in the period 1623 to 1631, and in those eight years the bishop, as the chronicle proudly informs us, had 900 witches burnt to death. He did this in the name of Christianity, in the name of morality, in the name of the law, and died under the delusion that he had performed good deeds.

We, who know that witches never existed, are

still today seized by a deep horror when we think of those unjustly executed wives and mothers.

In our great city of Berlin live two spiritual gentlemen, one of whom is named Philipps[87], the other Runze[88]. They say they are bearing witness to the teachings of the most honourable master, who spoke unto the people: 'He that is without sin among you, let him first cast a stone'.

Just as their predecessors saw the lame as marked, the mentally ill as possessed and the plague as the wrath of heaven, they see homosexuals as criminals and describe our struggle for homosexuals as 'nefarious shamelessness' (District Synod II Berlin, 17 May 1904).

They fancy that they are doing good work, just like the old prince-bishop Philipp, by demanding heavy penal provisions for homosexuals.

Now consider what I have told you about Berlin's uranians – and here I attest that it is all completely genuine – weigh it up in your conscience and your heart and decide if there is more truth, more love, more justice among those men of the church – who would certainly consider themselves quite free of guilt, or surely they would not be casting so many stones at homosexuals – or on the side of those who have no wish to see more victims of human ignorance, who, in accordance with the results of scientific research and the personal experience of many thousands of people, wish to finally see an end to the misjudgement and persecution which humanity will one day look back on as they do the witch trials of Philipp, the querulous Franconian bishop.

NOTES

¹ *Berlins drittes Geschlecht* (Berlin's Third Sex) was the third in what would eventually be 51 books in Hans Ostwald's *Großstadt-Dokumente* (Metropolis Documents), published between 1904 and 1908.

² The *Jahrbuch für sexuelle Zwischenstufen* (Yearbook for Sexual Intermediaries) was produced annually between 1899 and 1923. It was edited by Hirschfeld and issued by Max Spohr.

³ The place and date were omitted from later editions.

⁴ This is the first of a number of references in Hirschfeld's text to the classic style of Berlin apartment building which arose in the late 19th century, and continues to dominate the cityscape, which usually has at minimum a front block (*Vorderhaus*) and rear block (*Hinterhaus*) separated by a courtyard (*Hinterhof*). Later references in the text make the social distinction between those in the front blocks and those in the rear, and it is worth bearing in mind that as a rule better-off residents lived in the front block on the lower floors, with conditions generally worsening the higher and further back one lived in the building. At a later date, Hans Ostwald expressed his disdain for the 'man from the *Vorderhaus* who walks through the *Hinterhaus* with disgust'.

⁵ Karl Heinrich Ulrichs (1825-1895), the pioneer of gay identity and activism. Ulrichs coined the term 'uranian' (*Urning*) in the 1860s; it is a matter of dispute whether he inspired Britain's late 19th century/early 20th century Uranian poets to their label, or if theirs was a coincidental usage. Although Hirschfeld doesn't mention the fact here, Ulrichs also introduced the term 'homosexual' (*Homosexuell*) to German.

⁶ Kreuzberg and Wedding were both working class districts at the time of writing. The Scheunenviertel (lit. barn quarter) is a district to the north of Hackescher Markt in central Berlin which at the time of writing was

best known as a neighbourhood favoured by Jews who had emigrated from eastern Europe, and which was distinguished by poverty and overcrowding.

[7] The enormous police headquarters (*Polizeipräsidium*) stood at the corner of Alexanderplatz and Dircksenstrasse alongside an elevated railway. The building was heavily damaged in the Second World War and the site is now occupied by a shopping mall.

[8] The contemporary reader would have understood this to represent a markedly positive progression of life's fortunes, the east being generally poor, contrasting with the wealthy, haut bourgeois neighbourhood of Tiergarten.

[9] This, on the other hand, depicts a sharp deterioration in lifestyle; see note 4.

[10] This area was Berlin's preeminent nightlife quarter of the era, on and adjacent to Friedrichstrasse south of Unter den Linden, its approximate centre now occupied by the Checkpoint Charlie museum. This neighbourhood was covered in a later title in Ostwald's series *Lebeweltnächte der Friedrichstadt* (Friedrichstadt Nightlife, 1906). The southern end of Friedrichstadt around Hallesches Tor was a particular hub for gay activity, a fact not unrelated to the presence of barracks in the area. The designation 'Friedrichstadt' is less common in the present day.

[11] These are the first of numerous nicknames in Hirschfeld's text. Some associations defy translation, especially where they make reference to manifestations of subcultural phenomena never otherwise recorded.

[12] A designation for bands of young petty criminals borrowed from the Parisian underworld

[13] This is precisely the type of milieu covered in Hans Ostwald's *Dunkle Winkel in Berlin* (Dark Corners of Berlin, 1904), the first in the Metropolis Documents series.

[14] This is the first of numerous references to the paragraph in Germany's Criminal Code which read, in the version in effect during Hirschfeld's era: 'Unnatural fornication, whether between persons of the male sex or of humans with beasts, is to be punished by imprisonment; a sentence of loss of civil rights may also be passed'.

[15] A Berlin chapter of the YMCA was established in 1883; it was evidently as popular with gay visitors as its American equivalent.

[16] *Warmer Bruder* (lit. warm brother) in the original; *warm* was a slang term for gay commonly used in Hirschfeld's time. An associated term, *schwul*, derived from *schwül* (lit. humid, muggy), is the most prevalent term applied to gay men in contemporary German.

[17] This is one of numerous occasions where *Freund/Freundin* (lit. male friend/female friend) appears; each can also be translated as

'boyfriend'/'girlfriend' as the context dictates, although this is arguably an anachronistic usage. The translation deliberately retains the ambiguity of the original.

[18] 'Unnatural fornication' is taken directly from the wording of Paragraph 175; see note 14.

[19] A forested area on Berlin's western edge abutted, then as now, by a well-to-do residential district

[20] 'Es ist bestimmt in Gottes Rat', a setting by the composer of a poem on a theme of mourning and farewell by Austrian writer and philosopher Ernst von Feuchtersleben

[21] A passion for Richard Wagner's works was a widely acknowledged signifier of gay sensibilities in this era, both in Germany and elsewhere in Europe; in 1903 Hanns Fuchs issued the book *Richard Wagner und die Homosexualität* (Richard Wagner and Homosexuality) which questioned the orientation of the composer himself.

[22] There is a possibility (and only that) that this refers to steel magnate Friedrich Alfred Krupp (1854-1902), a friend of Wilhelm II who owned a hunting castle near Koblenz. Krupp's outing by the media and subsequent suicide in 1902 was the first great gay scandal of 20th century Germany. The episode described here is also a strange portent of a later incident; in 1908, Count Dietrich von Hülsen-Haeseler, the chief of Wilhelm II's military cabinet, danced for the Kaiser's amusement in a ballerina's tutu while the two were part of an aristocratic hunting party in the Black Forest. The count had a heart attack during this performance and died, so shocking the Kaiser that he fell into a nervous crisis lasting several weeks.

[23] Hirschfeld presumably means the work of this title (*Eine Vorlesung bei der Hausmeisterin*, 1860), which was in fact by Austrian writer Alexander Bergen, who in reality was Marie Gordon (1812-1863), a contemporary of Johann Nestroy. To expand on the gender-swapping theme, a photograph exists of Austrian Emperor Franz Joseph's brother, Archduke Ludwig Viktor (1842-1919), in drag for a role in Gordon's farce. In 1923, Ludwig Viktor was the subject of a pamphlet by Max Reversi which outed the recently deceased archduke; it was published by Adolf Brand.

[24] The pioneer of modern dance had established a dance school in Berlin the year this book was published.

[25] A waterway more or less defining the southern edge of central Berlin; at the time there was heavy commercial traffic on the canal, of construction materials in particular.

[26] Alexander von Humboldt, the distinguished Prussian naturalist and explorer, died in 1859 and August Wilhelm Iffland, if it is the Berlin actor to whom Hirschfeld refers, died in 1814, so presumably these at-homes lay some way back in the past.

[27] A German actor (1809-1871)

[28] 'There is no criminal offence if the perpetrator was in a state of unconsciousness or pathological mental disturbance which excluded him from the free exercise of will at the time the action was committed.'

[29] Like 'quiet, holy nights', this is a reference to a well-known German Christmas carol, 'O du fröhliche' ('O how joyfully/O how blessedly/Comes the glory of Christmastime!')

[30] A large hospital in central Berlin, still in operation

[31] Hirschfeld uses the term *Zwischenstufengewand*, the first part echoing the German title of his *Yearbook for Sexual Intermediaries*; see note 2.

[32] Thomas Koschat (1845-1918), Austrian composer. 'Verlassen' (Forsaken) is based on a Carinthian folk song ('Forsaken, forsaken, forsaken am I!/Like the stone in the causeway, my buried hopes lie./I go to the churchyard, my eyes fill with tears...')

[33] It is important to note that Hirschfeld uses 'pederasty' here in the legal sense it bore at the time, when it was essentially a synonym for sodomy.

[34] This was the association formed the previous year by activist Adolf Brand after his split with Hirschfeld and the Scientific-Humanitarian Committee.

[35] August von Platen-Hallermünde (1796-1835) was an aristocratic German writer whose homosexuality was relatively well-known, particularly after Heinrich Heine, provoked by Platen's anti-Semitic taunts, responded by outing him. Their bitter dispute was one of the great literary scandals of the Biedermeier era. A lengthy article on Platen that drew liberally from his letters to shed light on his sexuality was included in the *Yearbook* for 1904.

[36] **Author's footnote:** Näcke, P. Dr. 'A Visit to the Homosexuals of Berlin; with Commentary on Homosexuality. Archive for Criminal Anthropology and Criminality'. Volume XV. 1904. [Paul Näcke (1851-1913) was a German psychologist and criminologist who wrote extensively on homosexuality and introduced the term 'narcissism' to psychoanalysis. He was also a contributor to Hirschfeld's *Yearbook*.]

[37] Rudolf Presber (1868-1935) was a prolific German writer of literary and journalistic works, as well an early screenwriter. Here he writes in the 'feuilleton' format, a highly popular form in German newspapers to this day which presents first-person observations, frequently referring to different aspects of urban life or general questions about modern existence from the mundane to the profound. This article presumably appeared in the Berlin newspaper *Die Post*, where Presber was the feuilleton writer at the time. In 1907 Presber collaborated with Hirschfeld to publish the book *Aus eines Mannes Mädchenjahren* (Memoirs of a Man's Maiden Years), a pioneering first person account of trans identity by 'N. O. Body' (Karl M. Baer, born Martha Baer).

[38] In one of a series of autobiographical articles in the early 1920s for the journal *Die Freundschaft*, Hirschfeld notes that this was most likely

Hannemann's, a long-running gay establishment on Alexandrinenstrasse, Kreuzberg. This is where Hirschfeld met Otto de Joux (the pen name of Otto Podjukl, author of *Disinherited from Love, or the Third Sex*).

[39] Similar to a player piano, but with a greater range of sounds

[40] This may be Otto Müller, who played piano in various locales, dressed to varying degrees as a woman. He later opened his own tavern under the name 'Die schöne Müllerin', which feminised his own name while also alluding to Schubert's song cycle.

[41] From a later work in the *Metropolis Documents* series, *Lebeweltnächte der Friedrichstadt* (Friedrichstadt Nightlife, 1906, credited to 'Satyr', actually Richard Dietrich), we learn that the *chambre séparée* – originally nothing more than a private room in a restaurant – had acquired a reputation as a venue for prostitution.

[42] 'O, dass ich doch ein Räuber wäre', from the operetta *Gasparone* (1884) by Austrian composer Carl Millöcker

[43] La Belle Otéro (Caroline Otero), the Spanish dancer and courtesan who enjoyed enormous fame in Belle Époque France

[44] Here begins a long string of nicknames rendered as meaningfully as translation allows, although inevitably some wordplay is lost in the process. The examples in this paragraph combine a female name, often a diminutive, with an attribute. 'Blumenjuste', for instance, combines 'flowers' (*Blumen*) with the name Juste.

[45] This was the pen-name of Elisabeth zu Wied (1843-1916) who, as well as being a prolific writer, was also Queen of Romania.

[46] A reference to Cléo de Mérode, French dancer of the era; the original text transforms her name into 'Cléo de Marode', *marode* meaning ramshackle or dilapidated; this clever wordplay is sadly lost and the translation offered here is an approximation.

[47] The public urinals of Berlin at this time were rounded forms painted bottle green.

[48] This refers to the German proverb *Morgenstund hat Gold im Mund* (lit. The morning hour has gold in its mouth), equivalent to the English proverb 'the early bird catches the worm'.

[49] This establishment (lit. cat's mother), overseen by long-standing landlady Wilhelmine Techow, was located on Waterloo-Ufer, a stretch of the Landwehr Canal that was notorious for gay cruising. Paul Näcke (see note 36) also wrote about the Katzenmutter and the soldiers who prostituted themselves there. An anonymous book entitled *Das perverse Berlin* claimed in 1908 that 'a not insignificant portion of the history of homosexuality over the last two decades has played out in the Katzenmutter'. The building and almost all of its canal-side neighbours were destroyed in the Second World War.

[50] Now Mehringdamm, this street in Kreuzberg was frequently the scene

of military displays, with regiments marching from their barracks in the Hallesches Tor neighbourhood to the parade ground at what would later become Tempelhof Airport, and is now a park.

51 The Busch Circus had its own permanent venue in central Berlin at the time.

52 At the time of writing, this canal-side street abutted the now vanished Urbanhafen, a busy inland port for goods transported by barge (now a grassy slope in front of the Klinikum am Urban, a hospital). This, as well as a number of barracks within walking distance, lent the area a particularly raffish edge.

53 Here and in the next paragraph, see note 33

54 Hirschfeld's pioneering 1903/04 study based on a survey sent to students as well as metal workers; see Afterword

55 The Russo-Japanese war, still in progress at the time of publication

56 Leopold von Meerscheidt-Hüllessem, Criminal Director of the Berlin Police, was one such official who led 'tours' of foreign visitors around gay events and organisations.

57 **Author's footnote:** published 1904 in Paris by Albin Michet [Oscar Méténier (1859-1913) was a French writer who also established the Grand Guignol theatre and with it the confrontational horror for which it became a synonym. As well as *German Virtues and Vices: Berliners among themselves*, Méténier wrote a number of works that addressed the Parisian demi-monde in similar fashion.]

58 Fraternities at the time were much given to duelling, and the facial scars that often resulted were worn as a badge of masculine pride.

59 From Goethe's *Faust*

60 All three are characters from Friedrich Schiller's *Maria Stuart*.

61 Pastor Walter Philipps, a self-appointed guardian of moral order in Berlin at the time

62 The Russian city's bathing culture, including its gay subset, is covered in the later *Metropolis Documents* title *Pétersbourg s'amuse* (1907) by Viktor Günther.

63 This is most likely a reference to the Centralbad, a complex of Orientalist-themed baths where the Austrian Emperor's gay brother, Archduke Ludwig Viktor (see note 23), was caught propositioning a soldier. The site is now a gay sauna.

64 'Anyone who habitually or out of self-interest through his mediation or by granting or procuring the opportunity to abet fornication will be punished with prison for procuration; loss of civil rights or allowing of police control may also follow.'

65 These classified notices were 'inserted' into the book text on a double page, the men's notices on the outer left of the spread, the women's on the outer right; either the notices really were taken from newspapers or

the type was adapted to mimic their style.

66 Once a royal hunting domain, this large, landscaped park in central Berlin offers cruising areas to this day, although it is no longer a centre of prostitution.

67 These horseback constitutionals by Wilhelm II, in which he was often accompanied by one or more of his sons, were a popular postcard motif of the day.

68 In den Zelten was a street on the north side of the Tiergarten adjacent to the River Spree which was home to beer gardens and other outdoor pleasures spots. The unusual name ('in the tents') dates back to the era of Frederick the Great, when Huguenot refugees were temporarily housed here. After the First World War, Hirschfeld established his Institute for Sexual Science on In den Zelten in a building that was destroyed in the Second World War, along with all its neighbours. The site now abuts the grounds of the post-reunification Chancellery.

69 This is the only usage of the current common term for gay, *schwul*; see note 16.

70 This long string of underworld slang is extremely difficult to trace; some words are apparently Yiddish in origin while others are translated here with English colloquial approximations.

71 Tegel Penitentiary, in north-western Berlin, is still in existence and is now Germany's largest prison. The Plötzensee Prison, also in the north-west, was established in 1868 and became notorious in the Nazi era as a place not just of confinement but of execution, particularly of political prisoners. It is now a memorial, but a juvenile prison was established on part of the site after the Second World War and still operates today. The Rummelsburg Workhouse was established on the north bank of the Spree in eastern Berlin in the 1870s. The buildings have been transformed into private apartments.

72 At the time of writing, this memorial to the founder of the German Empire stood before the Reichstag; it now stands on the Grosser Stern where the Iron Chancellor can gaze up at 'Goldelse', the figure at the top of the Victory Column, who was similarly displaced.

73 These round advertising columns are a feature of the Berlin streetscape to this day. They were developed in the mid-19th century by Berlin printer Ernst Litfaß.

74 This, and the cabby's dialogue in the next paragraph, are delivered in Berlin dialect by which the contemporary reader would have placed the speakers among the working class.

75 Now Strasse des 17. Juni, this avenue extends the trajectory of Unter den Linden beyond the Brandenburg Gate, continuing on through the Tiergarten, over the Grosser Stern to the Charlottenburg Gate which marked the border with Charlottenburg, then a separate city.

[76] Leopold von Meerscheidt-Hüllessem (1849-1900) was the Criminal Director of the Berlin police whose duties included supervision of the city's gays and lesbians. As Hirschfeld's positive description indicates, his policy of monitoring rather than eradicating gay meeting places meant he was well regarded by the subculture.

[77] This refers to Friedrich Graf (Count) von Hohenau (1857-1914), a high-ranking Prussian officer. In a foretaste of the later scandals that would shake Wilhelmine Germany (in which Hohenau, his similarly inclined brother Wilhelm and Hirschfeld would all become entangled), the count had conducted a dalliance with a stable hand by the name of Aßmann. The two were given to travelling through the Tiergarten together in a closed carriage. Aßmann began demanding money, which Hohenau paid, the case only blowing open when other blackmailers emerged and insulted him in public. Although the case was heard in camera, enough details leaked out to force Hohenau to resign his post and retreat to the more sympathetic atmosphere of Italy.

[78] This was one of Meerscheidt-Hüllessem's operational innovations: the practice of keeping photographs of known criminals (mug shots) which could later be used for victims to identify them in the event of further offences. He was similarly pioneering in his use of fingerprinting.

[79] The existence of a list of known homosexuals in the city was mentioned as early as 1869 by Karl Friedrich Ulrichs.

[80] In 1904, the year that Hirschfeld was writing, the 16th Annual Assembly of the Morality Association convened in Cologne. It passed a resolution calling for the suppression of any groups or literature that campaigned for the repeal of Paragraph 175, and singled out Hirschfeld's Scientific-Humanitarian Committee by name, noting with alarm that it attracted 'thousands from the best-educated circles'.

[81] Hirschfeld here invokes a fairly obscure reference to the 1618 'Defenestration of Prague' which was judged to be one of the triggers of the Thirty Years War, specifically the protagonists Adam von Sternberg and Matthew Leopold (Dippold) Popel Lobcowitz. Why he should choose this among the countless other examples of violence he might have drawn from history is not entirely clear, although it may be significant that the defenestration was a revolt against the imperial order, and by rejecting this example Hirschfeld is perhaps signalling that his crusade is not aimed at the entire power structure as such.

[82] **Author's footnote:** *Pädagogische Zeitung*, 33rd Year, No. 33, Berlin, 18 August 1904, lead article: Education and the Third Sex, by Paul Sommer [Sommer was later a member of the Reichstag]

[83] **Author's footnote:** This committee, founded in 1897 with its headquarters in Charlottenburg, Berliner Strasse 104, has set itself the task of liberating homosexuals [the address in Berliner Strasse, now Otto-Suhr-Allee 93, was the location of Hirschfeld's apartment; the building is

gone but the location is marked by a memorial column].

84 **Author's footnote:** Note: as the lady mentions in a second letter, this close relation is her son. Of his blackmailers, the father as main instigator received a sentence of 2 years and 9 months, his twenty-year-old son, the 'friend' of the exile, 1 year and 9 months.

85 From the poem 'The Bride of Corinth' (1797)

86 Philipp Adolf von Ehrenberg (1583-1631); significantly, the witch hunts that Hirschfeld describes encompassed all strata of society, implicating even the highest offices.

87 Presumably Pastor Walter Philipps; see note 61

88 Presumably Walter Runze, author of such works as *With God for Kaiser and Empire!*

WHAT PEOPLE SHOULD KNOW
ABOUT THE THIRD SEX

I

Any person who can lay claim to a general education should take note of the petition included in this pamphlet, in which a very large number of Germany's most outstanding and renowned personalities call for the abolition of a sanction that applies not to criminals, but rather to a not inconsiderable class of people who are of a particular sexual disposition yet otherwise normal, whose existence and nature had eluded the attention of scientific research until just a few decades ago.

With this brochure, we are pursuing the goal of enlightening the broad public about this 'third sex', so that the widespread prejudice and erroneous beliefs that still prevail in this area might yield to proper judgement. In so doing we are also responding to a request by the head of the Reich Ministry of Justice, who said to Dr M. Hirschfeld[1], the President of the Scientific-Humanitarian Committee, in connection with this issue, 'Enlighten the public so that they will understand the government's motives when it removes this paragraph'. Those who read this little book conscientiously, without prejudice, will recognise that far from an endorsement of immorality, it represents instead a call for the removal of a grave injustice against unfortunates. May this pamphlet do its part to further invalidate the fear expressed by Ernst von Wildenbruch[2], one of the first signatories to the petition, when he wrote, 'I hasten to respond to the serious request that you have made of me, serious because I believe those who sign this appeal for the removal of the sanction expose themselves to the danger of slanderous speech, to persecution at the hands of stupidity and malevolence; nonetheless I believe it impossible not to sign this appeal'.

II

Everyone should be taught that every physical and mental quality generally regarded as manly is occasionally seen in women, and that everything in the structure and functions of the body that one ordinarily considers peculiar to women can, in exceptional cases, manifest in men. This leads to a wide range of intermediary stages between the fully formed persons of both sexes that one may summarise under the term 'third sex'. These transitional stages have been found not just in people of every race but also in every species where separate sexes are to be observed, and can be ascribed to the fact that differences between the sexes arise from greater or lesser development from one and the same base, sometimes failing to reach the customary level, sometimes advancing too far.

Here we offer an example to illustrate this more clearly. Prior to maturity, boys and girls exhibit exactly the same characteristics in their breasts, voice and hair coverage. It is only around the fourteenth year that we see disproportionate growth in breasts and hair in girls, and of the vocal cords and facial hair in boys, while the breasts and hair of the man, and the voice and facial hair of the woman, are halted in their development, or increase only in proportion with the rest of the body. But there are also not infrequent deviations from the average, thus boys and men with feminine breasts ('gynecomastics'), womanly voices ('falsetto singers'), womanly skin and hair qualities[3] and vice versa – girls and women with masculine hair coverage ('bearded ladies'), masculine voices and masculine appearance[4].

These sorts of transitional stages and inversions can be found in every other point of sexual difference, without exception. Along with physical hermaphrodites in the strict sense, these intermediary forms also apply to any man who is markedly feminine in his movements, inclinations or other characteristics (the effeminate) as well as those possessed of feminine sexual sensation, meaning those who, like women, can only love men (scientists call them 'uranians', 'homosexuals', 'counter-sexuals', 'perverts'; they are often popularly referred to as 'warm brothers'; there were similar names for 'those' people in Rome: *homo mollis*, or soft man). On the other hand this also applies to women with all manner of masculine attributes, drives and inclinations (men-women, while this also applies to many female emancipationists, female students, etc., although they may be unaware of it) as well as women with masculine sexual drives who, like men, can only respond sensually to women ('uranians', 'lesbians').

God, or nature, made these men-women and uranians alongside men and women, and the renowned Professor O. Schulze[5] rightly referred to it as 'downright comical that one should attempt to root out such natural qualities with pen and paper, or even restrict them in any appreciable way.'

III

Every parent should reflect that one or other of their children may be a uranian – as we will refer to those with same-sex inclinations, in keeping with the usage by Ulrichs – and that the aforementioned paragraph (175) could threaten their dearest one. Among those who have spoken out for the abolition of this law, there is a priest whom we are certain is himself unaware that one of his sons is a uranian. How many a mother is unable to comprehend why her son, despite his outstanding character qualities, despite true goodness of heart, is always so introverted, finds no joy in life until he one day does himself an injury, or why her daughter rejects one suitor after another. She would understand them were she to know something of the subject of this pamphlet, and would most certainly not neglect this point in her childrearing, in the choice of profession and marriage for her children. She would consider that for such children, marriage and procreation are unnatural acts, torture for those in question and a danger for their offspring, who are subject to all manner of mental and nervous disturbances.

There are primitive peoples who reserve certain professions for uranians, such as care of the sick, and permit their sons to wear women's clothing as soon as they are aware that they are men-women. Are these tribes not far more advanced than many civilized peoples in their understanding and sense of justice?

IV

It cannot be withheld from the public that the number of those born contrary, if still low in relation to the number of those normally inclined, is still too large for them to be housed in prisons, mental asylums or special institutions, for their right to existence to be denied, or for the state to demand that they kill themselves, emigrate or spend their lives suppressing one of the strongest of natural drives, a drive that scholars are not even agreed is possible to control in every case. There are uranians in the very highest and lowest levels of the population, in every class, the most highly educated and the least, in the cities as in the villages, among the most moral as among the most lax.

Anyone who knows these conditions will know in any case that out of a thousand uranians, hardly one is implicated, of fifty thousand incidents hardly a single one is investigated, and will also know that Bebel[6] was not incorrect when he said to the Reichstag (on 13 January 1898), 'If the infringements against Par. 175, which applies to thousands of persons from every level of society, from the lowest to the highest, were publicly tried, there would be a scandal the likes of which the world has never seen'.[7]

V

People should know that an inclination to persons of one's own sex does not arise – as is widely believed – through surfeit, self-abuse, seduction, depravity or fear of procreation; Dr Hirschfeld has never identified these causes among the almost 1200 cases that he has observed. On the contrary, in fact; most have done everything they can to rid themselves of this drive. They know the great dangers to which they are exposed, the shame that threatens to befall them, but the drive is stronger than their will.

Vienna's Professor von Krafft-Ebing[8], the most outstanding expert in this field, says that, 'Homosexual (i.e., same-sexed) sentiment can sometimes demand gratification with a force that renders mastery impossible'. As to the nature of this gratification, here too people hold utterly false beliefs.

But even for those who never act on these impulses, the existing law represents a grave charge and an insult, because it affects their holiest of holies – their love. The love for one's own sex can be just as pure, tender and noble as that for the other sex, differentiated only in its object, not its nature. These people are just as capable of outstanding achievements, as readily proven by a number of great men whose uranian nature can now be regarded as uncontested – Socrates, Michelangelo and Frederick the Great, to name just a few. As a sign of uranian poetry, we include a sonnet from the pen of Richard Barnfield[9], an English poet from the time of Shakespeare[10]:

> Sighing, and sadly sitting by my Love,
> He ask't the cause of my hearts sorrowing,
> Conjuring me by heavens eternall King
> To tell the cause which me so much did move.
> Compell'd: (quoth I) to thee will I confesse, Love
> is the cause; and only love it is
> That doth deprive me of my heavenly blisse.
> Love is the paine that doth my heart oppresse.
> And what is she (quoth he) whom thou do'st love?
>
> Looke in this glasse (quoth I)
> there shalt thou see The perfect forme of my faelicitie.
> When, thinking that it would strange Magique prove,
> He open'd it: and taking of the cover,
> He straight perceav'd himseife
> to be my Lover.

VI

Every normally inclined person should try, once, to put himself in the place of the uranian. It is a difficult, yet not unreasonable request. His inner life can be compared to one unjustly sentenced, who atones for a crime that he has never committed. He is of the unshakeable conviction that he is personally free of blame for his deviation, that it is nature that has played this trick on him, that he is entirely incapable of thinking and feeling differently. This unfortunate state, of which he is entirely innocent, is simply denied and regarded as vice by those who are incapable of imagining that a person may feel differently to themselves.

The creators of Par. 175 simply assume – and here the judges and the people follow their lead – that those who violate this paragraph are people just like themselves who of their own free determination have abandoned their natural inclination toward women to instead turn to men. They do not know that the uranian feels himself just as strongly attracted to his own sex as the legislator does to the other, that his disposition makes intercourse with women seem unnatural to him, that he is forced to love men all his life.

Almost all uranians are deeply unhappy, not because of their passion, which they find difficult to imagine themselves without, but because of the persecution, the social devastation, the loss of honour that they potentially face for that which the normal may allow themselves every day with impunity. This misjudgement and condemnation of their entire being arouses in them a great sense of bitterness. One need only think how much scorn a uranian young man may attract for merely giving expression to his feelings, without having ever committed a punishable act.

No, this paragraph does not protect that which is natural, as it intended, it fights it; it is not the deed but the law that is unnatural, unless one wishes to declare nature itself unnatural. We can no longer allow people who combine many of the character benefits of the man and the woman in themselves to be regarded as desecraters of human dignity.

VII

For the state and for society there is no option but to live with the third sex as far as possible, because it cannot be eradicated. In reality this is already the case today, as only relatively few have been taken by suicide, prison, asylums and hospitals.

One overestimates the power of the law if one believes it to exert an appreciable influence on the exercise of such a powerful natural drive. Criminal liability cannot suppress same-sexuality, nor impunity generate it; the repeal of the law has not increased the scourge in any land, nor has the existence of the paragraph reduced it. Bavaria and Hanover, where the uranian paragraph was suspended between the Wars of Liberation and the introduction of the Reich Criminal Code, offer visible proof of this.

That whole populations are enervated by same-sex love is a wholly groundless claim. It has been proven beyond doubt that it figured among the most powerful primitive peoples and was found in Greece and Rome as in other civilizations at the time of their rise, their apex and their fall.

On the contrary; the uranian, unsuited to starting a family, can be a valuable and productive member of society in many different areas of public life, and often is – despite his misfortune. Therefore one cannot regard him as parasitical or antisocial; one must instead come to an accommodation with him. If one may demand of a young woman that she protect herself from temptation without legal support, one can just as well demand it of a young man.

VIII

Every uranian should see it as his irrefutable obligation to struggle for his honour and his freedom, the highest goods that a person may possess. He should always remember the phrase of the great legal scholar von Ihering[11], who said, 'When one is denied a right, one must struggle and not yield; that is a moral obligation'.

The uranian should – and not just when he finds himself in the hands of blackmailers or involved in other such troubles – turn to the Scientific-Humanitarian Committee (address: Charlottenburg, Berlinerstr. 104), which has set itself the task of removing the prevailing criminal laws and prejudices. He should not be ashamed of his inclinations, but instead strive to refine his love and keep its sensual exercise to a minimum.

Here we expressly emphasise that we are not fighting against the requirements of the Christian moral code, whose ideals all should strive to fulfil, that we are only fighting for those who are clearly not equal to these ideals or must deny themselves in striving to fulfil them, that they not be branded as criminals by the state. Not only is this not a requirement of Christianity, it stands in sharpest contradiction to it.

The uranian should know that if he marries out of social or even monetary concerns, that while he may do so with impunity, he commits a grave wrong. Certainly forgoing matrimonial joy is a great renunciation, but bearing his heart to those who feel as he does can provide comfort and relief, and then he can at least bring spiritual, if not bodily fruits to ripeness in every area of human progress.

IX

Here we reproduce the submission to the legislative bodies of the German Reich setting out the main reasons for repealing Paragraph 175 of the Criminal Code. Of the more than 1000 signatures from the ranks of scholars, judges, doctors, clergy, writers and artists, space allows us to print just a few, but here we add that the committee can make the full list of names available on request.

'Paragraph 175 appears to be an anomaly

whose repeal may rightly be demanded.' Bishop Dr Paul Leopold Haffner[12], Mainz

To the legislative bodies of the German Reich,

Given that in the year 1869 both the Austrian and the German national health authorities, which included such men as Langenbeck and Virchow[13], submitted the appraisal requested of them which stated that the threat of conviction for same-sex intercourse should be lifted, with the justification that the acts in question differed in no way from other acts that had never faced the threat of punishment, that one could commit with one's own body or that women could commit with each other, or men and women between themselves;

With the view that the repeal of similar penal provisions in France, Italy, Holland and numerous other countries has in no way resulted in depravity or other unfortunate consequences;

In view of the fact that the scientific research that has engaged intensively with the question of homosexuality (sensual love for persons of the same sex) in the German-, English- and French-speaking territories within the last twenty years has without exception confirmed what the first scholars who turned their attention to the issue expressed, that this phenomenon which is widely distributed in time and location must, by its very nature, be the product of a deep internal constitutional disposition;

Emphasising that at present it can be regarded as all but proven that the causes of this phenomenon, so curious at first glance, are to be found in developmental conditions that are related to the bisexual (hermaphroditic) nature of man, which means that no-one should be ascribed guilt for such feelings;

Considering the fact that this same-sex disposition is just as insistent, if not more so, than the normal;

Given that according to the testimony of numerous experts, *coitus analis* and *oralis* (i.e., the sexual use of certain bodily orifices that ordinarily have other functions) is relatively rare in counter-sexual intercourse, at least no more widespread than it is among the normally sexed;

With the view that among those possessed by such feelings there are, it has been proved, not just in classical antiquity but in our times as well, men and women of the highest intellectual significance;

In view of the fact that the existing law has never freed a counter-sexual of his drive, but rather hounded many good, useful people, already amply disadvantaged by nature, unjustly into shame, despair, even madness and death, even where just one day of prison – the minimum sentence for this act in the German Reich – is mandated or even just in carrying out preliminary investigations;

Taking into consideration that these provisions have offered a great boost to the widespread practice of blackmail (*chantage*) and the highly reprehensible practice of male prostitution;

The men[14] named below, whose names stand guarantor for the gravity and integrity of their intent, inspired by the pursuit of truth, justice and humanity, declare the current formulation of Par. 175 of the Reich Criminal Code to be incompatible with progressive scientific findings and therefore call on legislators to amend this paragraph as soon as possible so that, as is the case in the aforementioned countries, sexual acts between persons of the same sex, just as those between persons of different sexes (homosexual as well as heterosexual) are punished only when they are carried out with the use of force, with persons under 16 years of age, or when they constitute a 'public nuisance' (i.e., when they violate Par. 183[15] of the Reich Criminal Code).

Anton Hermann Albrecht, minister and writer, Lahr

Dr Allfeld, Professor of Criminal Law, Erlangen

Dr A. Baer, Medical Consultant, Senior Physician at Plötzensee Prison, Berlin

A, Babel, Royal Senior Judge, Straubing, Bavaria

Ludwig Barnay, Privy Councillor, Wiesbaden

Dr Woldemar Freiherr von Biedermann, Privy Councillor, Dresden

Dr Bielefeld, Prussian Magistrate, Kehl am Rhein

Otto Julius Bierbaum, writer, Schloss Englar, Eppan

Black-Swinton, Councillor of Justice, Senior Public Prosecutor (ret.), Breslau

Dr Otto Brahm, Director of the Deutsches Theater, Berlin

Dr Heinrich Braun, Publisher of the Archive for Social Legislation and Statistics, Berlin

Hans Brendel, Military Court Councillor, Mainz

Dr Felix Friedrich Brück, Professor of Criminal Law,

Breslau

Dr von Burckhardt, Senior Medical Councillor,
Stuttgart

Dr Crédé, Privy Councillor, Chief Physician of
Carolahause and Surgeon General, Dresden

Dr J. Doutrelepont, Medical Councillor, Director of
the Dermatology Clinic, Bonn

Dr Albert Eulenburg, Medical Councillor and
Professor of Nervous Disorders, Berlin

Count Finkenstein, Herzogswalde

Fritzsche, District Court Justice, Zwickau, Saxony

C. August Förster, superintendent and former pastor,
Vienna

Dr Rudolf von Gottschall, Privy Councillor, writer,
Leipzig

Dr Gräfe, Medical Councillor and professor, formerly
Halle, now Weimar

Dr Agnes Hacker, Berlin

Dr Max Halbe, writer, Munich

Hennburger, District Court Councillor, Berlin

Dr E. Harnack, Professor and Director of the
Pharmacological Institute in Halle

Otto Erich Hartleben, writer, Berlin

Gerhart Hauptmann, writer, Schreiberhau

Dr Max Haushofer, Professor of Economics and
Statistics, Munich

Hessler, District Court Justice and currently City
Councillor, Berlin

Friedrich von Hindersin, District Court Councillor,
Saargemünd, Lorraine

Emil Hundrieser, Professor, sculptor, Charlottenburg

Dr J. Jastrow, private lecturer in political sciences at the
Berlin University

Hermann Kaulbach, professor and painter, Munich

Josef Otto Kerling, Royal Senior Judge, Esslach, Upper
Franconia

Dr G. Kleinfeller, Professor of Criminal Law, Kiel

Kormann, Imperial Magistrate, Thann, Alsace

Dr Richard Freiherr von Krafft-Ebing, Senior Professor
of Medicine, Royal and Imperial Privy Councillor,
Vienna

Kulemann, District Court Councillor, Braunschweig

Joseph Kürschner, Privy Councillor and professor,
Hohenhainstein

H. von Kupffer, Editor-in-Chief of the 'Berliner
Lokalanzeiger' Berlin

Eugen Landauer, District Court Councillor and
Magistrate, Stuttgart

Walter Leistikow, painter, Berlin

Dr Leppmann, Medical Officer, Royal Physician
and Medical Head of the Observation Institute for
Mentally Ill Prisoners, Moabit, Berlin

Max Liebermann, painter, Berlin

Dr G. Freiherr von Liebig, Privy Councillor and
Professor, Munich

Detlev Freiherr von Liliencron, writer, Berlin

Dr Franz von Liszt, Judicial Councillor and Full
Professor of Criminal Law, Berlin

Max Maier, pastor, Scheufling

Dr Masson, Senior District Court Councillor,
Frankfurt am Main

Dr Mendel, Professor of Nervous and Mental Illnesses,

Berlin

von Metternich, Councillor, District Councillor (ret.), Höxter

Dr Albert Moll, specialist in mental illness, Berlin

Muss, Prussian District Court Councillor, Mainz

Dr Näcke, Medical Officer, Royal Chief Physician at the Hubertusburg Mental Asylum, Leipzig

Dr Neisser, Medical Councillor, Professor for Dermatological and Sexual Diseases, Breslau

Albert Freiherr von Oppenheim, Royal Saxon General Consul, Cologne

Oppler, District Court Councillor, Metz

Dr Robert Otto, professor, Privy Councillor and Medical Councillor, Braunschweig

Peters, District Court Councillor, Mulhouse

Dr Julius Pierstorff, Professor of Political Sciences, Jena

Victor Freiherr von Reisner-Cepinski, writer, Charlottenburg

Curt von Rohrscheidt, District Court Justice, Danzig-Langfuhr

Paul Rothschild, District Court Councillor, Cologne

Professor Dr Max Rubner, Medical Councillor, Director of the Hygiene Institute of the Berlin University

Rump, Royal District Court Councillor, Traunstein (Bavaria)

Carl Sänger, pastor, Frankfurt am Main

Schrader, Magistrate, Stettin

Dr Freiherr von Schrenck-Notzing, neurologist, Munich

Dr Bernhard Schuchardt, Privy Councillor and Senior

Medical Councillor, Gotha

Dr R. Siemering, professor, sculptor, Berlin

Dr G. Sommer, Head of the Institute for Pathological Anatomy, Innsbruck

A. von Sonnenthal, court actor and Head Director, Vienna

Strössenreuther, District Court President, Fürth (Bavaria)

Franz Stuck, professor, painter, Munich

K. von Tepper-Laski, Cavalry Captain (ret.), Mönchsheim

Dr Th. von Thierfelder, Senior Medical Councillor and Professor of Internal Medicine, Rostock

Dr Georg Treu, Privy Councillor, Professor and Director of the Royal Sculpture Collection, Dresden

Dr Tuchatsch, District Court Councillor, Zwickau

Prof. Dr H. Unverricht, Medical Councillor, Director of the City Hospital Sudenburg, Magdeburg

Dr Julius Vargha, Professor of Criminal Law, Graz

Richard Voss, writer, Berchtesgaden/Frascati

Oscar von Wächter, Royal District Court Councillor, Kempten (Bavaria)

Felix Weingartner, Court Music Director, Munich

Dr Adolf von Wilbrandt, writer, Rostock

Dr Ernst von Wildenbruch, Legation Councillor, Berlin

Dr Franz Ritter von Winckel, Medical Councillor, Professor of Obstetrics, Munich

and many more.

Addendum to the petition

Further reasons invoked for the abolition of Par. 175 from a legal perspective and that also proved decisive for the repeal in Bavaria, France, etc.:

1. The paragraph contradicts the basic principles of the constitutional state, which may only punish where rights have been violated. If two adults commit sex acts in mutual agreement, in private, the rights of no third party are violated. Where rights are violated, other provisions apply.

2. The inquiries generally induce the nuisance that one seeks to control. Chauveau and Faustin Hélie, *Theorie du code pénal*, Volume VI, p. 110 offer the following justification for repealing the uranian paragraph: 'The avoidance of squalid and scandalous investigations, which so often turn family life upside down and themselves cause nuisance'. Only a very careful medical examination can determine whether the perpetrator is a born homosexual or – very seldom the case – not. But once the charge is raised the individual is already destroyed in society.

3. Moreover, the great difficulties that arise in enforcing the paragraph should be considered. Many capacities rightly emphasise that a law is no longer of value if no more than a vanishingly small fraction of occurrences are brought to court.

4. Furthermore, it should be noted that Par. 175 is so vaguely drafted that even among lawyers there are completely different opinions on what it covers. According to imperial court judgements, it covers not

only *immissio in corpus*, but also simple embraces and bodily friction; mutual onanism, on the other hand, is not defined by the law as fornication. 'This unfortunate law,' says Krafft-Ebing (*The Counter-Sexual in Court*, Leipzig and Vienna, p. 16), 'requires of the judge the most embarrassing determination of objective facts, that culminates in establishing whether friction took place or not, where the only witness is usually the passive party, often a blackmailer, a masculine hetaera, a thug who thinks as little of offering a false oath as he does of being sued for slander'.

5. Above all it should be pointed out that there is an *error legislatoris* here. In attaching the threat of punishment to the acts in question, the legislator was caught in a scientific fallacy which for him was the most essential reason for the threat of punishment. It can be assumed with the greatest certainty that he would not have pronounced this threat of punishment had he known of the fact of in-born contrary sexual perception, proven later. Similarly, the 'legal conscience among the people', which in the last revision of the Criminal Code was provided as the sole motive for retaining the paragraph, is based on three false assumptions. For one, the public was not aware that there are those who, despite all efforts to the contrary, feel only for their own sex, moreover they believe that this involves *immissio in anum* and the seduction of immature persons, whereas in reality pedication and the inclination to immature individuals is just as rare in counter-sexuals as it is in the normally sexed.

6. It has also been pointed out, not without

justification, that intercourse between men and between women, because it remains largely without consequence, should be of far less relevance to the rest of humanity than extramarital intercourse between man and woman, which is ultimately just as morally objectionable (one thinks, for example of the risk of syphilis, illegitimate birth, prostitution, etc.). The young man can defend himself just as well against seducers as the young woman. *Volenti non fit iniuria*[16].

7. Paragraph 175 drives hundreds to countries where uranian paragraphs no longer exist, robbing them of their fatherland and the fatherland of extensive intellectual and material means. The idea of being branded as criminals by nature itself, without the slightest guilt, makes most homosexuals immeasurably miserable and hounds many of them who have never harmed their fellow humans in any way, who have not even erred in the sense stipulated by Paragraph 175, to self-willed death (suicide for reasons unknown).

8. Finally, it must be emphasised that the paragraph makes it far more difficult to combat homosexuality and treat those afflicted with it, as they have an all too understandable reluctance to confess their sufferings, even to a doctor, if it might bring them into conflict with the Criminal Code.

[1] Although credited to the Scientific-Humanitarian Committee, this pamphlet was written by Magnus Hirschfeld who here refers to himself in the third person.

[2] German writer and diplomat (1845-1909)

[3] This was illustrated in the original by a photo of 'soprano singer W.W.', a man in elaborate drag in a formal portrait setting; this image was also reproduced in the 1901 *Yearbook for Sexual Intermediaries*.

[4] This was illustrated in the original by a photo of the French artist Rosa Bonheur (1822-1899) wearing something approximating late 18th century men's costume, an image also reproduced in the 1900 *Yearbook*.

[5] This was presumably the same Dr O. Schultze (sic) listed as a professor of biology at Würzburg in the full petition included in the 1899 *Yearbook*.

[6] August Bebel (1840-1913), the leader of Germany's first social democratic party, the progenitor of today's SPD

[7] Here Hirschfeld is paraphrasing Bebel's wording slightly. The SPD leader went on to say that the theoretical scandal would make the Dreyfus Affair, the Panama Canal Scandal and other public outrages 'look like child's play' in comparison.

[8] The renowned Austrian sexologist Richard von Krafft-Ebing (1840-1902), a signatory of Hirschfeld's petition

[9] English poet (1574-1620)

[10] The sonnet, number 11, was translated for a German readership in an elevated yet contemporary style.

[11] Rudolf von Ihering, also Jhering (1818-1892) was a law theorist. Hirschfeld uses this quote in his annual report for the 1901 *Yearbook*, with the note that it comes from the book *Das Kampf ums Recht*.

[12] The Catholic bishop of Mainz (1829-1899) was a highly cultured and socially engaged commentator who produced a range of literary and philosophical studies.

[13] German surgeon Bernhard von Langenbeck (1810-1887) and Rudolf Virchow (1821-1902), German medical polymath

[14] The list also included one woman: Agnes Hacker (1860-1909), a prominent early feminist who was one of the first German women to gain a doctorate.

[15] Paragraph 183 of the Reich Criminal Code, introduced in 1871, covered 'exhibitionist acts' and 'creating a public nuisance'.

[16] 'You cannot injure a willing person'

AFTERWORD

On 8 May 1868, Hungarian writer Karl Maria Kertbeny coined the word 'homosexual' in a letter to Karl Heinrich Ulrichs, the first gay activist in Germany, and indeed the world. A few days later, on 14 May, Magnus Hirschfeld was born in what was then known as Kolberg, a spa town on the Prussian Baltic coast (now Kołobrzeg in present-day Poland). The temporal proximity of these two unrelated events is remarkable. For Hirschfeld, sexual difference and the words used to describe it were, as the Germans say, 'laid in his cradle'. The investigation of sexual minorities, the development of a modern gay identity, the creation of a vocabulary to express its forms and activities, the struggle against social and legislative discrimination – these were to be the defining motifs of Magnus Hirschfeld's adult life.

Hirschfeld's large family formed part of Kolberg's small Jewish population. Father Hermann Hirschfeld was both a journalist and a doctor, dual disciplines echoed in his son's later academic pursuits of philology and medicine. During his studies, Magnus Hirschfeld co-founded Badenia Heidelberg, a student association (comparable to a fraternity) that represented the interests of Jewish students. This was an era in which anti-Semitism was transforming from age-old prejudice into modern political force, and right-wing nationalist groupings in universities and colleges liberally showered their Jewish fellow students with disdain. Not only did Hirschfeld's group refuse to ignore these slights, they frequently exercised the customary means of dispute resolution in this milieu – the duel.

All this was but a warm-up for the battle to come, one that would pit Hirschfeld against the moral order of German society. For while emancipation of Jews had been at least officially encoded in the constitution for the new empire in 1871, the first pan-German Criminal Code, also adopted that year, carried a proscription that directly addressed another element of Hirschfeld's identity. An inheritance from Prussian law, Paragraph 175 not only banned sexual contact between males, but placed it on the same level as bestiality (like the Victorians, Germany's legislators judged female homosexuality to be so fancifully improbable that it didn't even warrant state censure). The paragraph read, in full: 'Unnatural fornication, whether between persons of the male sex or of humans with beasts, is to be punished by imprisonment; a sentence of loss of civil rights may also be passed'. This piece of legislation, usually rendered as § 175 with the legal symbol found on standard German keyboards to this day, is cited hundreds of times in Hirschfeld's writings.

But it is one of the great paradoxes of the modern era that the German Empire, remembered as reactionary, bullish and bellicose, and which – in contrast with France and Italy, for instance – had outlawed male homosexuality, should give birth to gay identity as we know it. While liberalism was not at all a defining trait of the mainstream culture or its ruling elite, Wilhelmine Germany nonetheless sustained an outstandingly vibrant bourse of progressive, often radical thinking. True, official censorship was far from unknown and written works could be banned or confiscated, their creators sometimes fined or even jailed, but it is even more remarkable what passed through the net.

Hirschfeld's first publication, issued in 1896, is a perfect example. *Sappho und Sokrates* was credited to 'Dr. med. Th. Ramien' – revealing the status of doctor of medicine that Hirschfeld had attained four years earlier while otherwise concealing his identity. Its cover carries a Nietzsche quote ('That which is natural cannot be immoral') and the subtitle 'How do we explain the love of men and women for people of their own sex?'. Inside, the text opens with a mournful account of a gay man taking his own life, then goes on to discuss homosexuality as a condition with the use of charts and other empirical evidence, introducing a mix of personal testimony and scientific analysis that was programmatic for Hirschfeld's later publications. Here, as the title indicates, he is also setting out his stall by addressing both male *and* female homosexuality.

Sappho und Sokrates was published in Leipzig by Max Spohr (1850-1905), the first publisher in Germany, and most likely the world, to focus solely on gay-themed works. His list included a title by Otto de Joux, originally published in 1893, entitled *Disinherited from Love, or the Third Sex*. This may well have been the first German title to employ the term 'third sex' in something like the sense that Hirschfeld would come to use it, a term that would eventually dominate the country's discussion of gay and lesbian life around 1900.

Spohr was one of the co-founders when Hirschfeld brought the Scientific-Humanitarian Committee into being in his Charlottenburg apartment in 1897. This is generally acknowledged as the first gay rights association in history. Its aim was to enhance the status of homosexuals through scientific, social and legislative channels. So as well as research into the origins and expressions of same-sex attraction and the work of general public enlightenment, the Committee aimed specifically for the repeal of Paragraph 175.

It is important to acknowledge that while he was most certainly a pioneer, Hirschfeld had sympathisers in surprisingly high places. His most powerful ally was August Bebel, the patriarch of the German social democratic movement, the first politician in the world to speak up on behalf of gay emancipation. His centre-left party, of which Hirschfeld was a member, broadly supported repeal of Paragraph 175. In early 1898 Bebel stood up in the Reichstag to speak in favour of this change. 'If the police were to conscientiously carry out their duty,' he archly informed his fellow representatives, 'Berlin alone would have to build two new prisons, for this affects thousands of people from every social circle.'

Hirschfeld continued the hard, unpopular work of reversing centuries of legal opposition with his 1898 pamphlet *§ 175 des Reichsstrafgezetzbuchs: die homesexuelle Frage im Urteile der Zeitgenossen* (Par. 175 of the Reich Criminal Code: The Homosexual Issue as Seen by Contemporaries), again published by Max Spohr. It contained a petition which included over 250 names, bristling with titles – professors, lawyers, government officials. A large number of doctors offered their support, including a certain Müller, pointedly noted as having been personal physician to King Ludwig II of Bavaria. Among the signatories familiar to posterity were artists Max Liebermann and Franz (von) Stuck, writers Gerhart Hauptmann and Hermann Bahr, as well as the Austrian sexologist Richard von Krafft-Ebing. Also on board was Adolf Brand, who in 1896 had established the world's first gay periodical, *Der Eigene*. One particularly unlikely bedfellow among these names was Max Nordau, author of *Degeneration* (1892).

The following year, Hirschfeld greatly expanded his publishing endeavours in the form of the *Jahrbuch für sexuelle Zwischenstufen unter besonderer Berücksichtigung der Homosexualität* (Yearbook for Sexual Intermediaries with Special Consideration of Homosexuality), issued by Max Spohr, which would only cease publication in 1923. Each of these annual editions was a heavy tome filled with essays, scientific studies, first-person accounts, summaries of newspaper articles as well as reviews of publications both scholarly and literary. The title, the format and the publishing rhythm all suggested gravitas – these were not dashed-off tirades by malcontent pamphleteers, but rather weighty, considered pieces intended for an educated slash academic readership.

The 1898 petition was reprinted in the *Yearbook* with a far more extensive list of signatories, along with the full text of Bebel's speech of the same year. Bebel's inference that the police may have been turning a blind eye to the scale of gay activity in Berlin is especially piquant in light of an appreciative obituary included in the 1900 *Yearbook*. Its subject was Leopold von Meerscheidt-Hüllessem, the chief of Berlin's criminal police, who was tasked with maintaining order among the city's gay and lesbian population. His policy appears to have been one of relatively benign containment rather than open confrontation, an approach that was one of the largest single factors in the proliferation of the subculture that Hirschfeld would come to document in *Berlin's Third Sex*. But Meerscheidt-Hüllessem still kept this milieu under observation, and indeed would lead distinguished guests on tours of the city's gay nightspots. Hirschfeld, too, sometimes brought interested parties along on his own nocturnal forays, including writers Frank Wedekind and Herman Bang.

In 1901 we find Hirschfeld using the now modish term 'third sex' in the pamphlet *Was muss das Volk vom dritten Geschlecht wissen!* (What People Should Know About the Third Sex), included in this edition. This publication also included the 1898 petition in slightly altered wording. While the text is credited to the Scientific-Humanitarian Committee and there is a reference to Hirschfeld in the third person, we know the work to be Hirschfeld's own.

A number of the themes addressed in *Berlin's Third Sex* are already to be found here. Hirschfeld's strikingly forward-thinking text addresses readers with 'general education', with a direct entreaty to consider the lot of the differently sexed, to acknowledge their inclinations as an in-born condition, to consider even that one's own child might be among this group so spurned by the mainstream. The short text uses the effective rhetorical device of opening each section with a wide appeal ('Everyone should be taught...', 'People should know...'). Hirschfeld is keen to make the reader aware that there are far more 'uranians' than they probably realise. The appeal to both reason and sentiment that distinguishes *Berlin's Third Sex* is already apparent here. With its extensive print run and minimal purchase price – the equivalent of two standard postage stamps – it was, like the later work, intended to reach as broad a readership as possible.

At this point we should examine contemporary use of the term 'third sex' and consider precisely what Magnus Hirschfeld meant by it, although precision may be an over-ambitious goal; his use of the term is difficult enough to elucidate at any given point and also shifts throughout his writings.

Like 'uranian' and 'homosexual', it appears that the designation 'third sex' in this context was introduced to German by Karl Friedrich Ulrichs. A few years after Otto de Joux's 1893 title came a great wave of publications that made use of the term. An abridged list might include Elsa Asenijeff's *The Revolt of Women and the Third Sex* (1898), Ernst von Wolzogen's highly successful

The Third Sex (1899), Aimée Duc's *Are They Women? Novel of the Third Sex* (1901), M. Braunschweig's *The Third Sex* (1902), Rudolf Quanter's *Against the Third Sex* (1903), Senna Hoy's pamphlet *The Third Sex* (1904) and Johanna Elberskirchen's *The Love of the Third Sex* (1904). As the title of Rudolf Quanter's book makes clear, not all of these studies were sympathetic, and indeed amid this miscellany of fiction and polemics there was a wide variety of opinion on what the 'third sex' actually meant. Elsa Asenijeff, for example, applies the term to emancipated women.

What makes Hirschfeld's use of the label problematic is that he deploys it in at least three different senses – to men and women who desire their own sex and bear the characteristics of their assigned gender (homosexual), to those who become aware that they have been assigned the wrong gender (transsexual) and to those who exhibit physiological variations that place them at a remove from their assigned gender along a notional continuum (intersex). At times one senses a laborious attempt to superimpose one definition over another, with the suggestion, for instance, that lesbians and gay men were ipso facto intersex, a search for outward evidence of difference in fact confined to inner orientation. For a scholar who prided himself on his rigorous research methods, Hirschfeld had a surprising and dismaying susceptibility to the short-cuts offered by pseudo-science. In *What People Should Know...*, for instance, Hirschfeld makes the unsubstantiated claim that children born to members of the 'third sex' are prey to 'all manner of mental and nervous disturbances'. Any serious engagement with Hirschfeld's academic career must also confront his lamentable flirtation with the principles of eugenics and the egregious faux-discipline of 'racial hygiene'. But on the issue of the 'third sex', at least, we do well to remind ourselves that the terms for these phenomena and the theories behind them remain contested in the present day.

One signature absent from the 1901 work was that of Adolf Brand, who in 1903 split definitively with Hirschfeld and formed his own organisation, the 'Gemeinschaft der Eigenen'. It is a difficult name to translate, but the various English versions offered – Community of Self-Owners/the Self-Owned/the Elite/ the Special/the Self – all emphasise a sense of separation from the rest of society, inspired by philosopher Max Stirner's creed of individual anarchism.

This schism in the early gay movement was highly acrimonious and came with ad hominem attacks. Brand saw Hirschfeld as *altjüngferlich* – spinsterish – and had little time for his gradations of sexuality and gender. His Community insisted that one could present entirely as a man, with no obvious feminine qualities, and nonetheless feel attraction to one's own kind. So far, so modern, although it should be noted that they took little interest in lesbian love, or women in general. Also, the particular variety of man-love Brand advocated was far from contemporary, drawing instead on the ancient Greek model by which an older, usually married man would act as both mentor and lover to an adolescent. Brand himself was married, and saw no contradiction between this state and his activism.

Having claimed that there were far more homosexuals in society than was readily acknowledged, Hirschfeld set about attempting to estimate their number. To this end he sent surveys to students and metal workers, asking them to detail their sexual activities and inclinations. The questions alone were a provocation and in 1904 Hirschfeld was sued by a group of students, and even the Munich chapter of his Scientific-Humanitarian Committee distanced itself from his methods. Hirschfeld nonetheless published his findings in an extensive article in the *Yearbook*, which along with a wealth of statistical analysis, also considered the kinds of places that those attracted to their own sex might gather, and the lives they might lead. This study – which estimated the proportion of gays and bisexuals in society to be 2.3 per cent and 3.4 per cent respectively – is thought to be the first to address homosexuality that made use of survey data in this way.

Previously Hirschfeld had considered homosexuality in a general sense – as a condition, as a legal concern. In his survey we see him starting to shine the light of science on the concealed corners of gay life. But it was his encounter with Hans Ostwald (1873-1940) that would inspire him to truly address homosexuality as a lived experience, and a localised one at that.

Ostwald was a Berlin-born autodidact of astonishing industry with a vivid curiosity for the lives of those around him. He was particularly concerned with the marginalised members of Wilhelmine society, including the vagrant, the homosexual, the criminal, the bohemian, the occultist, the gambler, the radical, the wayward youth and – above all – the prostitute.

As the 20th century dawned on Berlin, its population was 20 times greater than it had been a hundred years previously. Ostwald recognised that the confounding pace of change and expansion, the kind that we see today in megacities like Mumbai and Lagos, had left the imperial capital a stranger to itself. The life of one's neighbours one street over could be as bewildering and unknowable as anything found in Germany's distant African colonies. Ostwald was interested in real living conditions in the modern city, the entire social structure from top to bottom, and the factors that led individuals, particularly the disadvantaged, to their stations in life. These preoccupations came together in his most ambitious and enduring project: the *Großstadt-Dokumente*, or *Metropolis Documents*.

The series targeted the same broad, educated yet non-academic readership that Hirschfeld had in mind for his *What People Should Know...* Although there were titles focusing on Vienna, Hamburg and St Petersburg, the majority were about Berlin. Between 1904 and 1908, Ostwald issued a total of 51 cheaply produced titles through the Hermann Seemann publishing house, which had recently moved from Leipzig to Berlin. It says much for Ostwald's compulsions and energies that he also wrote and published a ten-volume series of books on prostitution in parallel with the larger urban study.

The first of the *Metropolis Documents* was Ostwald's own *Dark Corners of Berlin* (1904), which explored the underclass in homeless shelters and the lowest of dive bars (the kind of marginal existences that

George Orwell would later investigate in *Down and Out in Paris and London*). It was followed the same year by Julius Bab's *Berlin Bohème*, which described a milieu barely more salubrious than that peopled by Ostwald's vagrants, but whose representatives wore their self-willed squalor as a signifier of artistic integrity. In fact it was a world not unfamiliar to Hirschfeld, who frequented bohemian taverns and numbered writers such as Else Lasker-Schüler among his friends. But these two titles were eclipsed by Hirschfeld's first contribution to the *Metropolis Documents*, and indeed none of the 48 titles that followed could match its impact or popularity.

'The great vanquisher of all prejudice is not humanity, but science,' announces Magnus Hirschfeld at the beginning of *Berlin's Third Sex*. Along with the public's desire to be scandalised or titillated by the sometimes gamey subject matter of the *Metropolis Documents*, Hirschfeld's status as a doctor was a key selling point. This deference to learned opinion may well be why Germany, with its reverence for scientists, academics and scholarly attainments, became the birthplace of modern gay consciousness. Hirschfeld presented same-sex attraction as just one in a spectrum of biologically valid variations, and while this was a far from uncontested approach, it surely made the journey to widespread societal acceptance a little easier.

For all this, *Berlin's Third Sex* is by no means a scholarly work. In contrast to his other contribution to Ostwald's series, in which Hirschfeld addresses alcoholism through liberal use of figures and tables, the evidence here is not empirical but anecdotal. And despite its later inclusion in the anthology *Das erotische Berlin*, there is a near total absence of sex. Those who picked up Hirschfeld's book ignorant of the logistics of sex between men or between women would have been none the wiser by the time they set it down. Hirschfeld has an opportunity to address a mass audience and win them for his programme of legislative reform, and he isn't about to alarm them with frank depictions of homoeroticism. Hirschfeld maintains that gatherings of lesbians and gay men are no more characterised by sexual encounters than any other form of social exchange. So determined is he to downplay the sex component of same-sex attraction that we begin to see the spinsterish qualities of which Adolf Brand complained. When Hirschfeld expresses disgust at the sight of bearded men in drag, he sounds more like an enemy of gay culture than one of its greatest champions. Overall, Hirschfeld's motives are too transparent, his appeal to sentiment too insistent, the tone too uneven for *Berlin's Third Sex* to be a wholly satisfying reading experience. But acknowledging its stylistic and structural flaws in no way diminishes the scale of its achievement. For this book is arguably the first truly serious, sympathetic study of the gay and lesbian experience ever written.

Hirschfeld estimates Berlin's gay population at 50,000. So much of what he reveals about the astonishingly extensive and diverse activities of this subculture – the word 'community' still feels premature here – seems to come from later eras. At the dawn of the 20th century we find distinctions between the effeminate 'queen' and the he-man homosexual, we find admiration for well-toned athletes, we find rough trade and sexual slumming, we find something like late 1980s New York voguing culture in the description of gay drag balls, we find gay parties starting up around midnight and continuing until dawn, we find butch, sporty dykes, we find cruising at the YMCA, we find coded classified ads and even a Grindr-like telegraph service by which one could order up temporary companions meeting various criteria.

Although he never outs himself, it must have been clear to readers of the time that Hirschfeld moved through this world not just as a sympathiser but as an initiate. There is an interplay of discretion and disclosure throughout *Berlin's Third Sex*. Sometimes Hirschfeld names venues and organizations, in other places enough information is provided that a knowing contemporary would have been able to piece the facts together. In compliance with Hans Ostwald's insistence that his writers consider the entire social construct, Hirschfeld depicts the lives of everyone from labourers, students and servants to the clergy, the military and the aristocracy, thus implicating the very pillars of Prussian propriety. Most inflammatory of all is the mention of a 'gathering of obviously homosexual princes, counts and barons'. Here Hirschfeld unwittingly foreshadows one of the great scandals of the Wilhelmine era, the 'Harden-Eulenburg Affair', one in which he himself would have a key role.

For all the exoticism, variety and difference Hirschfeld details in *Berlin's Third Sex*, one of the book's most dominant modes is sentimentality. A first person account by one young man focuses on romantic yearning rather than libidinal urges. It's long, it's mawkish, it could have been written by any sensitive young adult about a juvenile crush of either sex – and that's precisely the point. The sentimentality reaches its peak (or nadir, depending on your tastes) in a scene depicting an outcast gay son peering through the window of his family home at Christmas. But Hirschfeld also describes modest households where a son or daughter invites a same-sex lover into the family home, and it is this depiction of quietly unspectacular domesticity and familial acceptance which is perhaps most radical. Many readers, we can safely assume, would simply never have previously imagined the homosexual to have an emotional, non-sexual life, to have affections and romantic practices essentially indistinguishable from those of the heterosexual.

The crux of all this was that while dive bars, drag balls and late night beats would have seemed a world away to most bourgeois readers, here they were presented with the suggestion that homosexuality might very well cross their thresholds and alight on their settees, might already dwell among them in fact. Indeed Hirschfeld presents this as a direct question towards the end of the book, addressing the reader in the familiar, informal 'du' form.

The terminology throughout *Berlin's Third Sex* is unsettled. The 'third sex' of the title is barely to be found in the text, perhaps reflecting its fall from intellectual fashion; when he does use it Hirschfeld wraps it in qualifications. Hirschfeld picks up on Karl Heinrich Ulrichs' use of the term *Urning* (uranian), applying it to both men and women. It appears in either nominal or adjectival form just over a hundred times, but even more prevalent, with over 120 instances, is Ulrichs' other term *Homosexuell*, again either as a noun or an adjective. 'Heterosexual', an even fresher coinage, appears twice. 'Pederasty' is used here as a synonym for sodomy, and usually appears in a legal context. The most common term for gay in present-day German, *schwul*, appears only once, and with no supporting explanation, so too the adjective *warm*, its equivalent at the time, as well as *lesbisch*. Despite his focus on legislation targeting gay men, Hirschfeld is also greatly interested in the German capital's lesbians, discovering in them a self-confidence and diversity to rival their male counterparts. Hirschfeld was an avowed feminist, with links to Hedwig Dohm and other major figures of the women's movement, as well as those who stood at the intersection of lesbian and feminist activism, such as Johanna Elberskirchen.

Just as crucial as the names applied to modes of existence in *Berlin's Third Sex* are the names individuals give themselves, and they present any translator with significant challenges. Hirschfeld's subjects adopt an incredibly rich variety of camp pseudonyms, feminising male names (and vice versa), ironising, diminutising, making reference to in-jokes or popular culture now forgotten. These names are accompanied by any number of terms with which the gay subculture concealed its activities from the rest of society, as well as the specific guild patois of prostitutes and blackmailers. Anyone familiar with Polari, the gay dialect introduced to a broader public by the British radio characters Julian and Sandy in the 1960s, will find numerous parallels.

While a measure of nuance and suggestion is inevitably lost when transposing campy nicknames and underworld slang, even the common vocabulary in *Berlin's Third Sex* is charged. The terms *Freund/Freundin*, the male and female forms of 'friend', are highly ambiguous, suggesting both a companion in the English-language sense and a romantic partner. The gay literature of the time made deft use of this duality, with numerous references to 'friends', 'friendship' and 'love between friends'. With this single word one could hide in plain sight. It is consistently translated here as 'friend', but it should be clear from the context how it is to be understood.

We encounter this loaded term once again in the classified ads that Hirschfeld inserts into the text on a double-page spread in the original. Another recurring usage in these coded messages is *Verkehr*, which in the original can mean dealings, or exchange, but also intercourse. Likewise, we find the abbreviation *gleichges.* which could be short for *gleichgesinnt* (like-minded) – a heavy enough hint – but also suggests *gleichgeschlechtlich* (same-sex).

All of this served to inform the reader that whatever legislators or the average citizen might make of gay culture, it was happening anyway, right under their noses, to an extent they had never imagined. In his foreword Hirschfeld touches on the all-too prevalent belief that even acknowledging the lives of gays and lesbians constitutes 'propaganda' for homosexuality – we need look no further than Thatcher's Britain or Putin's Russia to see how tenacious *that* concept has been. But Hirschfeld was essentially a reformer, not a revolutionary. He sought not the overthrow of societal norms, but their expansion. The criminalisation of homosexuality, Hirschfeld claimed, benefitted no-one except the blackmailers for whom it provided a ready revenue stream.

Proceeding from the assumption that homosexuality is a biological imperative, Hirschfeld shows that denial of its expression is detrimental to society, injurious to the individual and – just as important – extremely difficult to enforce. He draws parallels between the witch hunts of the unenlightened past and their modern equivalents. He offers these thoughts amid a portrait of a gay subculture at the very beginning of the 20th century that assumes an extent and variety that almost defy belief. Ultimately, Hirschfeld's goal was to remove legal prohibition for that which consenting adults did with each other in private. Like so many visionary texts of the Wilhelmine era, *Berlin's Third Sex* foretells a world that eventually came to pass. For it is impossible for the modern reader in Western, industrialised society to encounter Hirschfeld's vision and not recognise in it something of the world in which we live.

Berlin's Third Sex was by far the most successful of the 51 *Metropolis Documents* titles, running into numerous editions. It was the subject of a seven-page review in the *Yearbook* which was – not surprisingly –

highly favourable. Hans Ostwald, perhaps emboldened by the book's sales figures, returned frequently to contentious figures in his series, including pimps, sect followers, socialists, unwed mothers and, inevitably, prostitutes. *Metropolis Documents* number 20 was a study of lesbians in Berlin (by Wilhelm Hammer, an associate of Hirschfeld), which might well have been expected to replicate the success of *Berlin's Third Sex*. But it was banned from sale, and Ostwald abandoned plans to cover even more inflammatory subject matter (child prostitution, sado-masochism). In 1907 came Hirschfeld's second and final work for the *Metropolis Documents*, *Die Gurgel Berlins* (Berlin's Gullet), his study of the city's alcohol consumption and its consequences.

That same year, Hirschfeld became entangled in the greatest scandal of the late Wilhelmine era. The 'Harden-Eulenburg Affair' was the umbrella name for a series of incendiary legal encounters that centred on claims, denials and counter-claims concerning homosexual cabals in the very highest imperial circles. The protagonists – initially, at least – were journalist Maximilian Harden and courtier Philip, Prince of Eulenburg, Kaiser Wilhelm II's closest friend, and the affair began when the former made mention of the latter's homosexuality in print. Hirschfeld's pioneering research and reputation as Germany's preeminent authority on homosexuality saw him called as a witness in two separate trials. The affair brought the issue of same-sex attraction to much greater public awareness, but not in a way that Hirschfeld might have hoped, and it is regarded as a contributory factor in the later collapse of the German Empire. Hirschfeld himself became a notorious figure known far beyond the rarefied world of sexology, and in 1908 a jaunty, scurrilous 'Hirschfeld Song' was immortalised in shellac. 'In all things he finds something concealed,' runs one line, meant as an insult to Hirschfeld's revelations which so discomfited wider society, but also a perverse tribute to his assiduous research.

Hirschfeld continued to publish, with a pioneering 1910 study of transvestites (a term Hirschfeld coined) followed in 1914 by his magnum opus, *Die Homosexualität des Mannes und des Weibes* (The Homosexuality of Men and Women), which ran to over 1000 pages, including some material reworked from *Berlin's Third Sex*. In the First World War Hirschfeld put his medical training at the service of the war effort, working as a field doctor, his initial enthusiasm for the war soon replaced by pacifism.

With the end of the war and the proclamation of the Weimar Republic, Hirschfeld opened the Institute for Sexual Science in Berlin. In 1919 he appeared in Richard Oswald's *Anders als die Andern* (Different from the Others), a film as radical in its sympathy for gay life as *Berlin's Third Sex* had been. It was one of a number of 'social hygienic' films of the era which were born of the same blend of prurience and enlightenment as Hans Ostwald's books, but it was soon banned. The following year Hirschfeld was attacked by right-wing thugs after a speaking engagement in Munich and so badly injured that he got to read his own obituary. Yes, the gay population of Germany and in particular

Berlin developed a confidence and openness that made it famous the world over, thanks in no small part to the efforts of Hirschfeld and his associates. But much as we remember the Weimar era as a time of sexual licence, it is important to note, for example, that half as many men again were charged for homosexual activity in the decade after the war as the decade before.

Throughout the 1920s, Hirschfeld carried on his research and travelled extensively, sharing his findings and speaking at a wide variety of events in support of gay men and lesbians and other sexual minorities. In 1929, Paragraph 175 came tantalisingly close to repeal after a government committee voted by a majority of one in favour of removing it. Even conservatives appeared to have acknowledged Hirschfeld's claim that the law was essentially unenforceable and of benefit only to blackmailers. But with the country sliding into crisis, the decisive Reichstag vote never came. For Hirschfeld himself, the growing menace of right-wing extremism made his position increasingly untenable. Gay, Jewish, feminist – he was trebly anathema to the Nazis, and received numerous death threats. Hirschfeld left for a speaking tour of North America and Asia in 1931 and never returned to Germany, instead settling in Vienna, then the Swiss town of Ascona, and finally Nice. Once the Nazis came to power in 1933 they attacked Hirschfeld's institute with predictable ferocity. It was not only his books and his decades of research that fell victim to the notorious Opernplatz book burning in May of that year – a bust of Hirschfeld was cast to the flames as well.

Magnus Hirschfeld died in Nice in 1935, on his 67th birthday. That same year the Nazis broadened the scope of Paragraph 175 and thousands who were arrested for violating the law would die in the camps. And unlike other legislation targeting minorities that had been introduced or intensified by the Nazis, it was not repealed after the Second World War, and well into the 1960s there were hundreds, even thousands of arrests for gay activity every year in West Germany. East Germany, meanwhile, had taken the surprisingly progressive step of ceasing prosecution for such offenses in the late 1950s. Although successively liberalized, Paragraph 175 was still on the statute books at the time of reunification, and only definitively repealed in 1994. By that time the German capital gave the impression of picking up where the Weimar era had left off, with globally renowned nightlife along with an astonishingly wide range of groupings and activities reflecting gay, lesbian, bisexual, transsexual, intersex and queer life in all its diversity. One hundred years after Magnus Hirschfeld felt the disdain of a nation during the Harden-Eulenburg Affair, his name was given to a riverside quay opposite Berlin's new Chancellery. And in 2017, 120 years after Hirschfeld formed the world's first gay rights association, the nearby Bundestag voted to allow same-sex marriage – the last major step in the march toward full civil equality for Germany's lesbians and gay men.